70 YEARS LATER

D-DAY

Remembering the Battle That Won the War

70 YEARS LATER

D-DAY

Remembering the Battle That Won the War

LIFE BOOKS

Managing Editor
Robert Sullivan

Director of Photography
Barbara Baker Burrows

Creative Director
Mimi Park

Deputy Picture Editor
Christina Lieberman

Copy Chief
Parlan McGaw

Copy Editors Don Armstrong,
Barbara Gogan

Contributing Writers
Douglas Brinkley,
John Keegan,
Daniel S. Levy

Writer-Reporters
Marilyn Fu,
Amy Lennard Goehner,
Mary Hart, Lina Lofaro,
Jane Bachman Wulf

Associate Picture Editor
Sarah Cates

Editorial Associate
Jehan Jillani

Consulting Picture Editors
Mimi Murphy (Rome),
Tala Skari (Paris)

TIME INC. PREMEDIA

Richard K. Prue (Director),
Brian Fellows (Manager),
Richard Shaffer (Production),
Keith Aurelio, Jen Brown,
Charlotte Coco, Liz Grover,
Kevin Hart, Mert Kerimoglu,
Rosalie Khan, Patricia Koh,
Marco Lau, Brian Mai, Po Fung
Ng, Rudi Papiri, Robert Pizaro,
Barry Pribula, Clara Renauro,
Vaune Trachtman

TIME HOME ENTERTAINMENT

President Jim Childs

**Vice President, Brand & Digital
Strategy** Steven Sandonato

**Executive Director, Marketing
Services** Carol Pittard

**Executive Director, Retail &
Special Sales** Tom Mifsud

Executive Publishing Director
Joy Bomba

**Director, Bookazine Development
& Marketing** Laura Adam

Vice President, Finance
Vandana Patel

Publishing Director
Megan Pearlman

Associate General Counsel
Helen Wan

Assistant Director, Special Sales
Ilene Schreider

Senior Book Production Manager
Susan Chodakiewicz

Brand Manager Roshni Patel

Associate Prepress Manager
Alex Voznesenskiy

Associate Project Manager
Stephanie Braga

Editorial Director
Stephen Koepp

Senior Editor Roe D'Angelo

Copy Chief Rina Bander

Design Manager
Anne-Michelle Gallero

Editorial Operations
Gina Scauzillo

Special thanks: Katherine Barnet,
Brad Beatson, Jeremy Biloon,
Dana Campolattaro,
Rose Cirrincione, Natalie Ebel,
Assu Etsubneh, Mariana Evans,
Christine Font, Susan Hettleman,
Hillary Hirsch, David Kahn,
Amy Mangus, Kimberly Marshall,
Nina Mistry, Dave Rozzelle,
Ricardo Santiago, Adriana Tierno

Copyright © 2014
Time Home Entertainment Inc.

Published by
LIFE Books, an imprint of
Time Home Entertainment Inc.
135 West 50th Street,
New York, New York 10020

ISBN 10: 1-61893-102-4

ISBN 13: 978-1-61893-102-3

Library of Congress Control Number:
2014930194

"LIFE" is a registered trademark
of Time Inc.

We welcome your comments and
suggestions about LIFE Books.
Please write to us at:
LIFE Books
Attention: Book Editors
PO Box 11016
Des Moines, IA 50336-1016

If you would like to order
any of our hardcover
Collector's Edition books,
please call us at
1-800-327-6388
(Monday through Friday,
7 a.m.–8 p.m., or Saturday,
7 a.m.–6 p.m., Central Time).

Endpapers: On the Arromanche beaches, Normandy. ALEXANDRA BOULAT/VII/CORBIS

Page 1: A squadron of Lockheed P-38 Lightnings under the command of Lieutenant Colonel Clarence Shoop flies across the English countryside on the way to France on D-Day. FPG/GETTY

Pages 2–3: General Dwight D. Eisenhower, Supreme Allied Commander in the European Theater, inspires the men of the 29th Infantry Division. U.S. ARMY SIGNAL CORPS/AP

These pages: On D-Day, June 6, 1944, American soldiers wade ashore at Normandy, facing heavy machine-gun fire. ROBERT S. SARGENT/CORBIS

D-Day in Our Day

**The shot heard round the world in Massachusetts? Gettysburg?
What was the crucial place and fight that allowed the United States to go forth and
become the land our Founding Fathers imagined? We must consider D-Day.**

WHEN HENRY LUCE FOUNDED LIFE magazine in 1936 he pledged in a red-blooded, nine-page, typed manifesto that the publication would answer a call: "To see life; to see the world; to eyewitness great events; to watch the faces of the poor and the gestures of the proud; to see strange things—machines, armies, multitudes . . ." Much later Luce said, looking back at the 1940s, "Though we did not plan LIFE as a war magazine, it turned out that way."

Of course it did. If the Great Depression had been the big story in 1936, quite quickly the events in Europe—those machines, armies and multitudes—were what needed to be shown. If you were showing life throughout the world from 1936 through 1938, you were paying attention to the sudden ascendancy of European Fascists, and of course the onrush of the German Nazis. And then, from 1939 through 1945, the war was your weekly story. LIFE did its job.

We did not plan LIFE as a war magazine, said Luce, but when war of such magnitude became the only story that mattered, we told that story as best we could. Our regiment of photographers increased. Some of them were shooters who were, to use a modern term, embedded. Some of them were actual soldiers who took pictures when they could. They saw war and experienced war. The photography from the front line of George Silk, a New Zealander, was riveting, and soon he was on the LIFE squad and covered fighting in Europe after making astonishing pictures in the Pacific Theater. On those islands Carl Mydans, one of our very first staffers, was captured along with his wife and word-side colleague, Shelley, and they spent part of the war in a Japanese POW camp. Carl's response would be that, after being freed in a prisoner exchange, he made the famous photograph of MacArthur wading ashore on his return to the Philippines, and then the visual document of Japan signing its surrender. W. Eugene Smith was critically injured in battle. Robert Capa, who was unscathed when going in with the first wave on D-Day, would later die while on assignment in a battle zone for LIFE.

Those stories will be told more fully in these pages, as will

the big story—D-Day, 70 years later. To recount the events of June 6, 1944—its action and importance—LIFE has asked one of the country's preeminent historians, Douglas Brinkley, to edify our readers, and he has certainly done that. Before his death in 2012, Sir John Keegan, who, like Brinkley, possessed not only great insight but a talent for nuance, wrote an essay for LIFE, reprinted here, describing the world stage on the brink of D-Day. Their words are surrounded by the images made by LIFE's platoon of photographers who were deployed in Europe in 1944—the men seen in the photograph here, and others such as the storied Margaret Bourke-White. She arrived in Germany and, marching forth with Patton's Third Army, documented the atrocities at Buchenwald and elsewhere.

D-Day is present in our day. That is the premise of our book. As Keegan points out, the Allies had fought for several years to achieve something approaching equilibrium. Now came D-Day, with no plan B, and whichever way the wind blew might determine the future of the free or not-free world.

As we worked on this book, it was interesting to us to find how very alive D-Day remains. Three members of our editorial team took great pleasure in being allowed to report on and write about some few things about the war—not least because we felt we were writing for our fathers. Writer-reporter Mary Hart's dad was in the first wave of the D-Day attack. Writer Daniel Levy's maternal great-grandmother was murdered in the Holocaust, and his father came into Europe on a secondary D-Day wave, then fought in the Battle of the Bulge, which he remembers today as, above all, frightfully cold. Managing Editor Robert Sullivan's dad also entered France after the first wave, and he remembered the confusion of the Bulge, though he would never talk about what he had witnessed at the liberation of Dachau. They and the others fought on, and they prevailed, and in the 21st century their sons and daughter are afforded the opportunity to pay them modest tribute.

Where might we be today without D-Day? Had it not been conceived, or had it not succeeded? That is a prospect altogether too chilling to consider.

In Service

Above: This band of brothers is made up of LIFE's combat photographers who would be covering the D-Day invasion. Standing, left to right, are Bob Landry, George Rodger, Frank Scherschel and Robert Capa. Kneeling are Ralph Morse, John G. Morris and David Scherman. Joining them in Europe would be colleagues George Silk, Margaret Bourke-White and others. This photograph was made in London just before Operation Overlord was launched. LIFE reported back from the beachheads immediately and continued to chronicle the fight in Normandy (and beyond) throughout the summer, autumn and winter of 1944 (opposite, our August 14 cover). At right is Private First Class Alan J. Levy. At far right is Master Sergeant Arthur C. Sullivan. LIFE has many ties to D-Day, and so do we all.

The War Before '44

To understand D-Day and all it represents as history's greatest, most emphatic comeback, it is important to understand what had already occurred.

By Daniel S. Levy

IT COULD BE SAID THAT THE ROAD TO D-DAY BEGAN TO BE paved 190 miles northeast of the Normandy beaches and 26 years before June 6, 1944. In late 1918, a 29-year-old corporal in the 1st Company of the 16th Bavarian Reserve Infantry Regiment who had been battling the enemy for four long years was at this point engaged at the Belgian front. He was a strange man; in his downtime he painted scenes of the battlefield, took care of a dog named Fuchsl, chatted about the evils of smoking, drinking and Jews—and loved the glory of the war. When injured by a shell blast during the 1916 Battle of the Somme, he had begged his lieutenant not to send him to a field hospital: "I can still stay with you, I mean stay with the regiment! Can't I?" During his time at the front, he won two Iron Crosses for bravery: the first one second class for having saved a seriously wounded officer in late 1914, the next a much more distinguished first class, rarely issued to a corporal, which he received for "personal bravery and general merit" after capturing a group of Frenchmen in August 1918.

This corporal was Adolf Hitler, and in October 1918 he was fighting near Ypres when mustard gas blinded him. "My eyes were like glowing coals." It took a few weeks before "the burning pain in the eye-sockets had become less severe," and while he was convalescing, a local pastor walked into the military hospital. "Trembling" from the news he had come to deliver, the clergyman announced there was going to be an armistice the next day, and Germans now needed to "trust to the magnanimity of our former enemies." Hitler was stunned. "I broke down completely," he wrote seven years later in his memoir *Mein Kampf.* "It was impossible for me to stay and listen any longer. Darkness surrounded me as I staggered and stumbled back to my ward and buried my aching head between the blanket and pillow." Hitler found himself blind again, and he wept for the first time since the 1907 death of his beloved mother. But then "a miracle came to pass." His sight was restored. It was then that he received a "supernatural vision." Voices called to him. They told him to save Germany. The revelation made him dream of building a Germanic empire that would rival the glories of Rome. Thus was he propelled upon his political rise; thus started his murderous march toward World War II.

In 1919, the Great War's victors negotiated peace in a treaty at Versailles, France. While America's President Woodrow Wilson, with his idealistic Fourteen Points, dreamed of creating a peaceful world where nations determined their own futures, others, including Prime Minister David Lloyd George of Great Britain and French premier Georges Clemenceau, demanded severe punishment. The partitioning of land and drafting of reprisals began. Germany lost Alsace and Lorraine to France, had to give up control of the Rhineland, saw parts of itself cut off to re-create Poland and

The Seeds of the Axis

On the previous pages we see American soldiers aboard a small landing craft during the opening hours of Operation Torch, the Allied invasion of Vichy French–controlled—which is to say German-controlled—western North Africa in 1942. By this point, all the lines have been drawn. From 1939 to 1941 the Nazis flirted with the Soviet Union but then double-crossed them, and the Allies would ultimately coalesce around three major powers—the U.S.S.R., Great Britain and, last in, the United States—while the Axis would be Germany, Italy and Japan. (There were other nations involved, to be sure; it is too linear to draw a world war so narrowly, but there it is.) The Axis leaders came from enormously different backgrounds, and their countries had varying histories and grievances. On the opposite page, we see Adolf Hitler in two photographs taken during the First World War, his moustache grander than the trademark version. He is in his field uniform at left, and with two other soldiers and his beloved dog during a stay at a military hospital in Pasewalk in 1914, at right. At left on this page is the Japanese emperor, Hirohito, in his enthronement ceremony robes in 1928; how much power he had in relation to his military is a subject of debate, but he will be the man to announce to his country the surrender declaration two decades hence. Below is Italian prime minister Benito Mussolini reviewing the ranks of 200,000 Fascist Blackshirts in Rome in 1925. He will be hung upside down after his execution. As these photographs indicate, the world was in play immediately after World War I, and well before America entered the fray.

witnessed the emergence of such new nations as Yugoslavia and Czechoslovakia. Germany was prevented from creating an *Anschluss,* a union, with Austria. Its military was emasculated, its fleet was reduced, and advanced weaponry like military submarines, aircraft and tanks were deemed verboten. The monetary penalties were set at about $63 billion (not adjusted for inflation). And then there was Article 231, which required Germany to accept blame—guilt—for the war.

Hitler, who even when young showed traits of megalomania (one schoolteacher in Linz, Austria, recalling him as "argumentative, willful, arrogant, and bad-tempered . . . notoriously incapable of submitting to school discipline"), seethed. What he considered the betrayal of Versailles pierced his heart, and in 1919 he joined the 40 members of the newly formed German Workers' Party. It was a magnet for those like Hitler who were dissatisfied with the new Weimar Republic's parliamentary democracy. By 1921 he had become chairman, and the party was renamed the National Socialist German Workers' Party—the Nazis— and had attracted such like-minded people as Ernst Röhm, Alfred Rosenberg, Rudolf Hess and Hermann Göring. Its members believed that the Germans were the highest race, the Jews were "a parasite within the nation," the leaders who accepted the peace at Versailles were "November Criminals," liberal democracy was a sham and Marxism was the enemy.

Germany was not alone in shifting to radical conservatism. In Italy, Benito Mussolini, a former schoolyard bully, had also served in World War I (like Hitler, rising only to the rank of corporal). In 1919 he founded the *Fasci di Combattimento*, fighting leagues that became known as the Fascist Party, and, presenting himself as "a man of the people," won the support of unemployed veterans. He believed that only a dictator, "a man who is ruthless and energetic enough to make a clean sweep," could cure the nation's ills. Hoping to be such a leader, Mussolini organized his followers into Blackshirts squads: armed thugs who terrorized their communist, republican, unionist and Catholic enemies, killing hundreds. His party helped form a coalition

government in 1921. But wanting more, they marched the following year on Rome, where King Victor Emmanuel III asked Mussolini to form a new government. Once in power, Mussolini dismantled the democracy, turned Italy into a dictatorship and dubbed himself *Il Duce*, the Leader.

In the East, Japan had been industrializing since the Meiji Restoration of the 1860s. Similarly filled with a sense of their racial and social superiority, the Japanese dreamed

The Rise of the Nazis

In the United States in our own day there are what are called "country club prisons" for white-collar and other non-hard-core criminals, and this seems to be the kind of penitentiary the lederhosened Hitler (opposite page, far left) and his well-attired comrades are ensconced in after their unsuccessful 1923 coup. To the future Führer's left in this picture at the prison in Landsberg am Lech are Emil Maurice, Hermann Kriebel, Rudolf Hess and Friedrich Weber. Once they are freed, their ascent to power, fueled by their countrymen's feeling of disenfranchisement and also a tattered economy, would be relatively swift; by 1938 the annual swearing in of SS men in Berlin would grow to the extraordinary spectacle below.

of expanding their realm. They flexed their martial muscles, winning wars against China (in 1895) and Russia (in 1905) and, in 1910, annexing Korea. When Hirohito assumed the imperial throne in 1926, he was considered quasi-divine and granted supreme authority by the Meiji Constitution, but in fact he possessed little power. The conservative leaders were truly in control, and they fiercely opposed westernization and hoped to enlarge Japan's sphere of influence in Asia and elsewhere.

THE GERMAN ECONOMY, BATTERED BY AFTERSHOCKS OF the war and the reparations, was in shambles. Extremists began calling for an end to the Weimar Republic, and Hitler believed this was the time to strike. On November 8, 1923, a large crowd converged on the Bürgerbräu Keller, the Citizen's Beer Hall, in Munich to hear a speech about the need for a dictatorship. Göring then barged in with brown-shirted storm troopers. Hitler hopped on a chair, fired a gun and announced, "The national revolution has begun." The day after the Beer Hall Putsch, a battle broke out between Hitler's supporters and the police; three officers and 16 Nazis were killed. Hitler scurried off but was soon arrested, and while he proclaimed at his trial that "there is no such thing as high treason against the traitors of 1918," the court sentenced him to five years at the Bavarian fortress of Landsberg am Lech. While imprisoned with Hess, Hitler

started to write *Mein Kampf* (*My Struggle*). The first volume, called *The Settlement of Accounts*, deals with his childhood, the war, the loss of 1918, the greatness of the Aryan people and their need to "care for the purity of their own blood." It is rife with anti-Semitic and nationalistic rants, bizarre social Darwinism and fantasies about the need for *lebensraum*, living space in the east. Volume two, *The National Socialist Movement*, lays out what the Nazis must do to create the Germany of his dreams. The book is a clear handbook for power and terror, the secular bible of Nazi Germany, and by the start of the war had sold 5.2 million copies.

Out of prison within nine months, Hitler consolidated his power. He became a mesmerizing orator, using simple, staccato and impassioned speech patterns, and attracted many followers. The Nazis rose, first at the ballot box, but then—and more quickly—through the use of violence. In the election of 1933 the Nazis and their allies won the vote and then passed an enabling act that gave Hitler dictatorial rule. They crushed the opposition, disbanded trade unions, arrested liberals and Jews, and banned and burned books— from Hebrew and Yiddish prayer books to the writings of Thomas Mann, Ernest Hemingway and Helen Keller. In 1934, Hitler combined the presidency and the chancellery, making himself *der Führer*, the leader.

This was the start of the Third Reich, what Hitler saw as the successor to the Holy Roman Empire and the

The Horror Begins

The Beer Hall Putsch certainly indicated the Nazis were not only audacious but violent, and *Kristallnacht,* a pogrom (or series of planned attacks, the results of one of which are seen on the opposite page) on November 9 and 10 of 1938 showed that, vis-à-vis the Jewish population, the Nazis were keen on being killers as well. Some 90 Jews died in Germany and Austria in the attacks, and 30,000 were rounded up and sent to prisons and concentration camps. As to these latter places of incarceration (and so often, death), the Germans needed more of them, and needed them more geared to the purpose. At left, we see Heinrich Himmler visiting a building site in Poland, where one of the most infamous camps, Auschwitz, is rising. Below: Jews are under arrest in Warsaw, Poland, during the German invasion. Women, children: This mattered not.

The War Before '44

German Empire of 1871 to 1918. Hitler envisioned his own empire lasting 1,000 years. For this, he needed Germany to be strong, and Hitler started to rearm the Fatherland. While the League of Nations, an organization for international cooperation, had been set up at Versailles to keep the peace, it lacked power. Appeasement was the way. The nations of western Europe were deeply war-averse after the carnage of the First World War, which saw the death of nearly 9 million—Britain alone had lost 900,000, France more than 1.3 million—and many leaders assumed that if the Nazis got what they wanted they would stop. So as Hitler ignored Versailles, the German air industry boomed from 3,000 workers when he took over to 250,000 in 1939, and cranked out 3,000 warplanes a year. Militarization brought full employment, which in job-strapped Germany made the Führer enormously popular, and turned the average German citizen into an easy and willing player in the Nazi's pathological beliefs and murderous plans. Mussolini meanwhile tested the military waters. In 1935, Italy invaded Ethiopia. The League of Nations could do nothing. When Hitler's troops retook the Rhineland the following year, there was condemnation, but no action was taken.

Japan was also expansionist. The island nation lacked sufficient land for agriculture, and was resource poor, its growing population in need of such basics as oil, iron and coal. The ultranationalists eyed Manchuria across the Sea of Japan. Instead of any hoped-for era of enlightenment and peace, the Dark Valley, a time of militarism, aggression, repression and censorship, ensued. The Japanese, too, encountered little opposition, for the Chinese were engaged in a long civil war between Chiang Kai-shek's Nationalist forces and Mao Zedong's communist troops, making the nation weak and ripe for the taking. This is important to note in relation to D-Day, when all these tables were emphatically turned: In the mid-1930s, the Nazis, Fascists and Japanese ultranationalists saw a world that looked ripe for the picking—and it was. It would take a decade of struggle and death for that world to find its strength, shore up its will and prevail.

Japan also looked to western-controlled Indochina, Malaya, the Philippines and the East Indies for resources. Watching the growth of Japan, Hitler spied a chance to counterbalance the Soviets to his east, and in 1936 signed with the Japanese the Anti-Comintern Pact. The world was off balance and pushed over the edge in July 1937 when Japanese troops near Beijing confronted Chinese soldiers at the Marco Polo Bridge and helped set off World War II. They invaded Beijing and Tianjin, headed to Shanghai, entered Nanjing and helped themselves to needed resources. Hitler sought a stronger alliance with Japan, and in September 1940, Germany, Italy and Japan signed the Tripartite Pact, forming the Axis alliance and promising "to assist one another with all political, economic and military means if one of the three Contracting Powers is attacked."

The New World War

In this dramatic photograph, German soldiers are invading Poland during the *Blitzkrieg* offensive of September 1939. On August 22, a bit more than a week before the assault was launched, Hitler had unequivocally declared his intentions to his top aides: "The aim of this war [is] . . . in the enemies' physical elimination. That is why I have prepared, for the present only in the East, my 'Death's Head' formations with orders to kill without pity or mercy all men, women, and children of the Polish race or language. Only in this way can we obtain the living space we need." Ultimately, it is estimated, roughly 5.7 million Poles died in the war. On September 1, the Germans pushed in, and though the Poles mounted desperate resistance, within five weeks it was over. The Soviets began the sovietization of the parts of the nation they were granted under their alliance with Germany, and Berlin took the rest. How quickly Hitler turned his eyes elsewhere has been confirmed by history: quickly, indeed. Meanwhile, nations around Germany finally acknowledged Hitler's rapacious expansionism and steeled for the fight with differing degrees of will. France would fall, Britain would not.

ITLER MEANWHILE MOVED TO FULFILL HIS DREAM OF unifying the German people. In March 1938 he sauntered south, and Austrians ecstatically welcomed his troops in what was known as the War of Flowers. Hitler needed the resource-rich east, and called for retaking from Czechoslovakia the "ethnically German" Sudetenland.

There was a sense in the west that the Germans had some legitimate complaints, one being the loss of a million of its citizens when the Versailles treaty carved up their territory. And now, many hoped that there would be peace if they gave Hitler what he demanded. Yet there were voices like that of England's Winston Churchill, who warned against concessions. The appeasers, though, drowned him out, and in September 1938, British prime minister Neville Chamberlain headed to Munich with the hope of preventing a general European war. In the Munich Agreement, Chamberlain and the French premier Édouard Daladier gave Germany the Sudetenland, and Chamberlain returned to the British Isles a hero, announcing that he had achieved "peace with honor" and "peace for our time."

Churchill called the agreement "a total and unmitigated defeat," and was near the truth when he said, with his customary sense of drama and eloquence, "England has been offered a choice between war and shame. She has chosen shame and will get war."

For while Hitler said he had no further territorial demands,

he wanted more, and he took more of Czechoslovakia in March 1939. He also wanted purity. Beginning in 1933, following Hitler's ascension to power, the Nazis established concentration camps to remove—preferably permanently—enemies of the state and other "undesirables" from society. Among the first prisoners were Roma (Gypsies), Jehovah's Witnesses, homosexuals, "subversives" and political dissidents. The regime also targeted artists and intellectuals and the mentally and physically handicapped. In another effort to "purify" the country, the Nazis had been ratcheting up their campaign against the Jews, from business boycotts to the firing of Jewish government workers, with Joseph Goebbels, the minister of public enlightenment and propaganda, working to make sure "the era of extreme Jewish intellectualism is now at an end." Back in September 1935, the Germans had passed the Nuremberg Race Laws, which denied Jews citizenship and the vote. One of the laws, the Law for the Protection of German Blood and German Honor, denied them the right to marry non-Jews. Then in early November 1938, Goebbels and Reinhard Heydrich orchestrated the "spontaneous demonstrations" called *Kristallnacht*. During the Night of the Broken Glass, firefighters and policemen stood idly by and watched as rioters burned and damaged more than 1,000 synagogues, destroyed 7,500 businesses, attacked Jewish homes, hospitals, schools and cemeteries and murdered some 90 people. Afterward the Germans arrested

GRANGER

JOHN TOPHAM/BLACK STAR

The Blitz

Several places, including Poland, underwent *Blitzkrieg* attacks by the Germans. But in Britain, the serial bombing of 16 cities from September 7, 1940, to May 21, 1941, will forever be known as "the Blitz." The term is from the German word for lightning, and certainly the sky was lit every night: London was attacked 71 times in 36 weeks; Birmingham, Liverpool, Plymouth and Bristol were hit, and so was Glasgow in Scotland. What had ignited it? Certainly, Hitler's desire for world domination represented the principal match. But in fact there had been a different spark. In late August 1940, German night bombers went astray and missed an English airfield, dropping their bombs in the center of London, hitting several homes and killing civilians. Churchill, enraged, started bombing Berlin, and wouldn't quit that effort until well after D-Day four years later. London (left, the Battersea area being toured by the prime minister in 1940) got by far the worst of the Blitz. The city was bombed for 57 consecutive nights. Children and women were sent from the city to safer harbors in the countryside, and on the opposite page we see children sheltering in a farmer's field. The amazing thing: The Royal Air Force outdid the Luftwaffe in the Battle of Britain, and the Blitz was not a success for the Nazis. Their march had been stalled. The war was on.

America Is In

President Roosevelt was impressed by the British defiance of the Nazis and inspired by Churchill's devotion to turning back the tide. But he could not effectively turn public opinion in his own country without a catalyst. The Japanese would supply that on December 7, 1941—the "date which will live in infamy"—by bombing Pearl Harbor in Hawaii. It is interesting that the rash act—the wakening of the sleeping giant—was not Hitler's. If Pearl Harbor had been inspired by his impulsiveness in Europe, so be it. As Hitler did with Poland and France, and wanted dearly to do with Britain, the Japanese behaved as if their initial, brutal onslaught was the end of the game. Left: Japanese pilots listen to radio broadcasts from Honolulu just before the attack. (At least, that's the story from a Japanese propaganda film made in 1941.) Below: The USS *Arizona* burns before sinking into the harbor on December 7. Opposite: President Roosevelt signs the declaration of war on the eighth, his onlookers cognizant of the moment.

30,000 Jews and shipped them off to the concentration camps as well, with Göring quipping, "I would not like to be a Jew in Germany." The Germans blamed the Jews for the violence and fined the Jewish community 1 billion reichsmarks ($400 million), confiscated their property, banned them from schools, parks and resorts, and Göring proclaimed that there would soon be a "final reckoning with the Jews."

Even while the west appeased Germany, some prepared for a fight. Starting in the 1930s the French erected the Maginot Line, a series of forts, weapons and obstacles that stretched from Switzerland to Luxembourg to keep the Germans out. Chamberlain ordered the speeding up of the British rearmament program, set up radar stations along the coast and established shadow factories that could quickly convert to war manufacturing.

Hitler had turned his attention to Polish lands, while Mussolini in April 1939 took over Albania. The next month the two leaders signed the Pact of Steel alliance to support each other when war arrived. Britain and France vowed to back nations like Poland as events unfolded. Hitler, though, gambled that neither England nor France would actually go to war over Poland; to make sure that an invasion would not drag in Russia and create an eastern front, he shocked the west on August 23 when German foreign minister Joachim von Ribbentrop signed a nonaggression pact with the Soviet Union. A day later the British signed an Anglo-Polish pact.

Then in the early hours of September 1, 1939, war in Europe came in a *Blitzkrieg*, brought by the German air force. The Luftwaffe's "lightning war" rained bombs on Polish villages and towns. Terrorized citizens fleeing the explosions slowed down the movement of defending troops. The Germans quickly destroyed most of the Polish air force, and as Junkers Ju 87 dive-bombers (better known as Stukas) eliminated defenses, Panzer tanks smashed through and troops swarmed in. On September 3, France and Britain declared war, yet by the eighth the Panzers had massed outside of Warsaw. On the seventeenth the Soviets crossed into Poland, and on the twenty-seventh Poland surrendered. Germany and Russia then hungrily divided up the land.

In April the Germans swarmed into Denmark and Norway. And while the French braced themselves along the Maginot Line, on May 10 the German army simply passed around it, going through the hilly and wooded Ardennes Forest of Belgium, rushing through with tanks as Messerschmitts and Stukas took out defenses. Holland surrendered four days later and Belgium after two weeks. French soldiers surrendered in droves.

As Chamberlain's government started to shatter, Churchill was made First Lord of the Admiralty, and on the day that the Germans invaded the Low Countries, Chamberlain resigned and Churchill took over as prime minister. With Neville Chamberlain, England had shied from a fight. With Winston Leonard Spencer Churchill, they had a scrappy aristocratic

bulldog and romantic patriot. The son of Tory politician Lord Randolph Churchill and Jennie Jerome, the beautiful daughter of a New York financier, Churchill had attended the Royal Military College, Sandhurst, fought in India and the Sudan, covered the Boer War as a journalist—during which he was captured and made a daring escape from a military prison—and headed to Parliament in 1900. Endowed with a boyish charm that softened his self-assured arrogance, he started serving as First Lord of the Admiralty in 1911, but lost that post after the disastrous campaign at Gallipoli in the Dardanelles in World War I. He then joined the army and saw combat in France with the 6th Royal Scots Fusiliers. Churchill spent the 1930s, what he called his "wilderness years," futilely warning members of Parliament of Nazi growth and the need for British rearmament. Now that he was prime minister, they listened to the man with the iron constitution who was determined to fight to the death for the sake of civilization.

There was much to do. In Churchill's first speech to the House of Commons, on May 13, the new prime minister vowed that Britain would never give in to the Nazis, saying, "I have nothing to offer but blood, toil, tears and sweat," and assuring the assembled members that the only aim for his nation was "Victory, victory at all costs, victory in spite of all terror, victory, however long and hard the road may be; for without victory there is no survival." But the Nazi onslaught continued, and in the Foreign Office, Sir Alexander Cadogan was quite prescient when he noted that "we must lose the war for three years before we win a decisive battle."

That is a helpful estimation, for here we must scurry ahead, as our book is about D-Day. So much happened in this interim that we cannot detail here, but surely Hitler was

THOMAS D. MCAVOY

off and running. The retreat from Dunkirk, the fall of France: all of it. Now, however, we hope our readers have an understanding of the seeds of World War II, and we continue on.

As GERMANY PLANNED A CROSS-CHANNEL INVASION OF England, the British braced for the worst. In June 1940, in one of his many wartime speeches, Churchill exhorted his countrymen and vowed not to surrender, saying, "We shall go on to the end. We shall fight in France, we shall fight on the seas and oceans, we shall fight with growing confidence and growing strength in the air, we shall defend our island, whatever the cost may be. We shall fight on the beaches, we shall fight on the landing grounds, we shall fight in the fields and in the streets, we shall fight in the hills; we shall never surrender, and even if, which I do not for a moment believe, this island or a large part of it were subjugated and starving, then our Empire beyond the seas, armed and guarded by the British Fleet, would carry on the struggle, until, in God's good time, the New World, with all its power and might, steps forth to the rescue and the liberation of the old." If his listeners were inspired, their will was tested on July 10 when the Germans swooped in and the Battle of Britain began, with the Luftwaffe flying 1,300 bombers and dive bombers and 1,200 fighters to take out shipping and ports and then air bases, radar stations and aircraft factories.

Fortunately, the British advanced radar system was efficient, and squadrons of Hawker Hurricanes and Submarine Spitfires took out their enemies in the sky. Churchill told Parliament, "Never in the field of human conflict was so much owed by so many to so few." When the Germans accidentally dropped some bombs on civilian London, the British countered with an attack on Berlin. That bombing so enraged Hitler that he ordered the devastation of Britain. German bombers blanketed not only the capital but other cities like Liverpool and Coventry, taking out whole residential blocks. But as people hid and searchlights swept across the sky, the prime minister rallied the populace, flashing his V-for-victory sign, visiting antiaircraft batteries and fighter headquarters, consoling the newly homeless and telling the nation that this was truly "their finest hour." The British not only repulsed the German onslaught, but the Nazis suffered more airplane losses—1,773 to Britain's 915—and the British resupplied their fleet faster than did their enemy.

Hitler abandoned his plans for invasion, but he kept up the bombing, hoping to cause the British to buckle and petition for peace. As thousands of Britons cowered in shelters and Underground stations, the bombs incinerated docks and dwellings. Eighteen-year-old Len Jones recalled how on September 7, the first day of the Blitz, "bombs began to fall, and shrapnel was going along King Street, dancing off the cobbles . . . the suction and the compression from the high explosive blasts just pulled and pushed you . . . you could

actually feel your eyeballs being sucked out. I was holding my eyeballs to try and stop them going. And the suction was so vast, it ripped my shirt away, and ripped my trousers. Then I couldn't get my breath, the smoke was like acid . . . And these bombers just kept on and on; the whole road was moving, rising and falling."

The bombs did not discriminate, hitting even Buckingham Palace. An explosion destroyed the chapel and the courtyard on September 13, and King George VI and Queen Elizabeth had to race to the shelter, with the queen afterward saying, "I'm glad we have been bombed. Now I can look the East End in the face." The Blitz stretched into the middle of 1941 and resulted in the deaths of more than 30,000 people.

It wasn't just cities being targeted. German submarines, *Unterseeboote,* or U-boats, prowled the Atlantic, sinking ships at will. At the end of 1940 the German Admiral Karl Dönitz initiated the "wolf pack" tactic, where groups of U-boats, avoiding sonar by surfacing at night, attacked ships. German sailors fondly called this the "happy time," but for Allied sailors and passengers, it was terror. Lieutenant Commander Otto Kretschmer, the "Wolf of the Atlantic," aboard *U-99* wrote in his diary after a group of U-Boats attacked a convoy in October, sinking 20 ships out of 35, "The destroyers are at their wits' end, shooting off star shells the whole time to comfort themselves and each other . . . I am now beginning to pick them off from astern of the convoy." The attacks endangered the delivery of supplies, raw materials and food to Britain from the U.S. and Canada. This could have meant starvation and defeat. Churchill later admitted that the effect of the U-boats was "the only thing that ever really frightened me during the war." The British learned to deal with the wolf packs by arranging an escort system. It also helped greatly that they had cracked the Nazi's Enigma cryptographic system, which relied on a complicated encoding device with 60 wheel orders and 17,576 rotor settings that allowed operators to scramble messages into theoretically unbreakable combinations. With captured machines and codebooks and the use of early computers, a British team of mathematicians, scientists and even chess masters, working at Bletchley Park outside of London, figured out the Enigma, Lorenz and other codes, and through the intelligence gathered were able to decipher U-boat communications, which enabled convoys to navigate safely.

Churchill was keenly aware of how precarious the state of Britain was, and this son of a British lord and an American socialite hoped that those in the New World would come to his country's aid. But America wanted no part of the war. The U.S. had lost 116,516 servicemen in World War I. While this was just 5 percent of what Britain and France had lost, it was too much for a nation with a wide streak of isolationism that went back to George Washington, who near the end of his presidency had warned of entanglement in European politics

Rosie the Riveter and Her Sisters

These are two photographs that appeared in LIFE, which was covering the home front as well as the action "over there." Above: Women working in a steel mill in Gary, Indiana, who had been hired in 1942 to replace men "called to duty"; and, at right, a pilot in the U.S. Women's Air Force Service, which ferried supplies domestically, in 1943. "Rosie the Riveter" became a cultural icon and source of pride once America entered the war, and the potential of our post-Depression industrial output was realized: We had many people eager to work, and now we had a cause. Discoveries were plenty as women filled in for men: They could do anything. In 1942, Kay Kyser, a big-band leader of the time, had a big hit with "Rosie the Riveter"; in Canada, Veronica Foster— "Ronnie, the Bren Gun Girl"—was Rosie's counterpart. Women played baseball while men were away, they built airplanes, they flew airplanes. It has been claimed that Rosie was the Eve of American feminism, but that is seen as a claim too far by many sociologists. A more interesting question, perhaps: Was there a real Rosie? Well, there was Rosalind P. Walter, a Long Island, New York, aristocrat who worked the night shift building the F4U Corsair fighter. And there was Rose Will Monroe, who was an actual riveter at the Willow Run Aircraft Factory, in Ypsilanti, Michigan, building B-29 and B-24 bombers. And there was . . . Well, it doesn't matter. There were so many Rosies. Heroes all.

and affairs. America felt safe, buffered by the two great oceans that separated it from Europe and Asia. And while Americans felt a familial link to Great Britain and generally supported the British fight, there were also vocal German sympathizers rooting for the other side, most prominent among them the famed aviator Charles Lindbergh, who had been a guest of Hermann Göring's at the 1936 Berlin Olympics and had spoken often of his admiration for the Nazis.

However, Churchill knew he had a sympathetic ear and an ally in Franklin Delano Roosevelt, and he cultivated the relationship. Roosevelt declared that while the U.S. would remain neutral in law, he could "not ask that every American remain neutral in thought as well." Like Churchill, Roosevelt came from an old patrician family. The Roosevelts, who had arrived from Holland in the 17th century, were prominent in business and politics. FDR's distant cousin was President Theodore Roosevelt, a leader who reveled in American power and exceptionalism; Roosevelt's wife, Eleanor, was also related to Theodore. Educated at Harvard and Columbia, Roosevelt served as an assistant secretary of the Navy under President Wilson during the First World War. He advocated for a strong navy and the increased use of submarines. He contracted polio in 1921, but he was determined not to let the crippling disease stop him and won the New York State governor's office in 1928, and in 1932, early in the Depression, the presidency. Once in office he widely expanded the powers of the presidency to deal with the unprecedented financial disaster, instituting his New Deal programs to get Americans back to work, and by 1940 he was seen by much of the country as a visionary leader.

The Eastern Front

In this picture taken by a German photographer in July 1941, we see an infantry squad advancing into a small Russian town that had already been softened by Luftwaffe bombing during an operation called Barbarossa. It's important to understand the Eastern Front (the German term) as we approach D-Day. Once Germany and the Soviet Union had fallen out—and that is a mild term for the dissolution of their wartime alliance—the Axis was at war with the U.S.S.R., Poland, Norway and others in central and eastern Europe. We know what happened to Poland; Norway would not be a factor. And so in the east, it was the Soviet Union, led by Joseph Stalin, who had been betrayed by Hitler. (Such a tyrant might have understood a tyrant?) The fighting on the Eastern Front, if taken in its totality from 1941 until 1945, remains, even today, the largest on-ground military battle in history. The tolls are best measured as inconceivable—20 million of World War II's 60 million dead—the causes of all that killing too sad to consider in toto, but ranging from the bullet to starvation to the death march. The Soviet Union would be pressing in from the east when D-Day was finally launched, but what had occurred on the Eastern Front—the denial of Moscow and Leningrad and the shift in momentum, the push back, the march to Berlin—would be deemed, by history, crucial.

The War Before '44

If Congress had tied his hands, the Neutrality Act allowed the President to give supplies to foreign lands if they were paid for. On September 2, 1940, FDR signed the "Destroyers for Bases" agreement, turning over 50 old destroyers to the British in return for 99-year leases on territory in Newfoundland and the Caribbean that America could use for air force and naval bases. The British could not afford the ships, so Roosevelt proposed the Lend-Lease Act, which skirted the rules and allowed the U.S. to give away tanks, planes, trucks and food if their use was necessary for American security. At that time

TSUGUICHI KOYANAGI

The War in the Pacific

It had officially started for the United States with the attack on Pearl Harbor, and it would not be thoroughly ended until well after D-Day with the Japanese surrender. Meantime, there were ferocious battles to be fought and much blood to be spilled. The war in the Pacific Theater, as it was called, did affect the strategies and deployments in Europe. As we will learn, when Britain tried to push its will and turn D-Day into a Mediterranean Sea invasion, America used the Pacific chip—*we'll go fight there*—to force its own will. But even more importantly: Britain couldn't help much in the Pacific and the Soviet Union hadn't at all (though Stalin said it would, if Operation Overlord succeeded). The Australians and New Zealanders were brave, but their forces were limited. Above: In 1942, American prisoners of war embark upon the barbaric Bataan Death March after having been captured by the Japanese on their way to Corregidor in the Philippines in 1942. Opposite: The bodies of Americans who have been killed on Buna Beach, New Guinea, in 1943. When this photo was made for LIFE by George Strock, there was a ban on American publications' showing any dead U.S. servicemen. LIFE's editors appealed to the White House, and Roosevelt, agreeing that complacency had set in among the populace, said: Run it. LIFE did, and the photo had the desired, galvanizing effect. *Let's go win this thing.*

FDR also announced that America would be the "Arsenal for Democracy" and help arm and support Europe and China in their war against the Axis nations.

In retaliation for bombing England, the British set out to strike terror into the enemy and crush their spirit. The British Chiefs of Staff ordered Arthur "Bomber" Harris to carry out "area bombing" of cities, and Churchill's scientific adviser, Oxford professor Frederick Lindemann, determined that strategic bombing would make a third of all Germans homeless in 15 months. Vickers Wellington planes equipped with "Gee," a new radio-navigational aid, illuminated potential targets with flares, following this up with incendiary bombs and then high-explosive bombs for ultimate damage. They attacked Lübeck in March 1942 with 400 tons of bombs, incinerating the wooden buildings of the medieval town. In late May, a thousand planes flew over Cologne and turned the air white and red with flames. In July 1943, RAF Avro Lancaster four-engine bombers set out with new and highly accurate bombsights in Operation Gomorrah. When they and American B-17 Flying Fortresses arrived over Hamburg, their bombs destroyed shops, docks and factories. The wind fanned several small fires in the area, and the flames united, drawing in the surrounding air and creating 150 mph walls of fire. Children and old people were sucked into the flames. Those who had made their way to shelters were incinerated, baked and suffocated there. Forty-four thousand people were killed and a million were left homeless. George Orwell satirized the military policy by writing, "Berlin Bombed: Babies Burn." The point, though: In the years well before D-Day, Germany was on the march, but the fight was well and truly engaged.

AFFAIRS DID NOT QUICKLY UNRAVEL FOR NAZI GERMANY throughout the first half of the 1940s, but they changed in steps. Hitler had made an alliance with the Soviet Union, but all Joseph Stalin had to do was read *Mein Kampf* to know what the German leader really thought of communism. Hitler saw the Slavic lands as a place to expand into, a source of slave labor—too tempting for the Führer to pass up. Operation Barbarossa, named for the medieval Holy Roman emperor, was Hitler's dream of conquering Russia. He believed that unlike Napoleon and the German forces in World War I, he could win decisively and win quickly, that all he had to do was "kick the door in and the house will fall down." The attack was launched in June 1941, and Nikita Khrushchev, who would take over following Stalin's death, in 1953, recalled that Stalin was so surprised by the German attack that he was initially paralyzed into inaction. But the Soviet leader quickly rallied his nation. This son of a poor, sadistic cobbler and a devout washerwoman from the Georgian town of Gori had a will as determined and brutal as that of Hitler. As a young man he read Karl Marx and the writings of Vladimir Ilyich

GEORGE STROCK

Lenin, and he joined the Bolsheviks in 1903. Stalin, a stocky man with jet-black hair and a face scarred by a childhood bout with smallpox, ruthlessly rose to power, outmaneuvering and crushing his rivals. After Lenin's death, in 1924, he oversaw the industrialization of his nation, brought about the collectivization of millions of farms, ended personal freedoms, terrorized citizens and purged everyone he deemed a threat—from party bosses to military leaders.

Hitler let his desire to create his grand *Reich* lead him into Russia. This was not western Europe but a vast land with inadequate roads, a place of which French novelist Victor Hugo wrote: "Cruel winter came like an avalanche. After one white plain, another white plain." The German invasion started well on June 22, 1941, as Russian forces crumbled; that morning the Nazis destroyed more than 1,000 grounded planes. The Germans took Minsk on the twenty-eighth, and as the Luftwaffe raided and tanks blazed, they started bombing Leningrad in September, an attack that turned into an 872-day siege. Starvation gripped the land, and civilians ate dogs to survive. When they ran out of dogs, they consumed rats, black peat and crows. When those sources dried up, gangs grabbed lone pedestrians and resorted to cannibalism. By October, when 3 million Soviet soldiers were already prisoners, the Germans launched Operation Typhoon against Moscow, sending nearly a million German soldiers, 14,000 guns and 550 planes against the Soviets' 1.25 million men, 7,600 tanks and 1,000 planes. Stalin remained in the capital, organized the defense, and to show his resolve even orchestrated a grand military display in Red Square on Revolution Day. As the Germans bombed Moscow, women and children worked to make defensive shelters, 8,000 citizens were executed for perceived cowardice, and Stalin assigned "blocking detachments" to execute deserters. The Germans made it to within 15 miles of the city and then stopped. For while the German invasion initially made headway, it had been poorly planned. The men lacked winter clothes, and the vehicles didn't have antifreeze. The Soviets counterattacked and started to drive the Germans back. At the start of the invasion, Churchill took to the airwaves, pledging support for the Russian people and stating that "the Russian danger is . . . our danger."

As things went poorly for the Germans in Russia, the Japanese made their own grand master-race grabs. Their aggression against their Asian neighbors caused the United States in early 1940 to not renew a commercial treaty it had with Japan. Then followed an American embargo on iron and fuel. Publicly, the Japanese scoffed at these western moves, bragging of their own Greater East Asia Co-Prosperity Sphere—essentially a play for a Japan-centric empire. They eyed Southeast Asia, the Philippines and Malaya for their oil and minerals and as locations for military bases. Knowing that grabbing these lands would lead to war with America, they decided that they had to knock the Americans out of the game, and saw the destruction of the American Pacific fleet as a way to buy time. There were clear clues as to what the Japanese were planning. But general blundering, bad communications and inept interpretations on the part of the Americans meant that the U.S.—which had broken Japanese codes and had even been warned by Joseph Grew, the American ambassador in Tokyo, who passed on intelligence predicting an attack—did not see what was coming.

When it came, it flew in on two destructive waves. On the morning of December 7, 1941, Admiral Isoroku Yamamoto launched torpedo bombers, dive bombers, horizontal bombers and fighters at the U.S. naval base in Pearl Harbor, Hawaii. In just two hours, 350 planes from the Land of the Rising Sun sank two battleships, damaged six others, destroyed 188 aircraft and damaged another 159, and killed 2,042 Americans. Yamamoto hoped that the attack would destroy the U.S. fleet and force America to seek peace, thus allowing Japan unfettered way in Asia. But three American aircraft carriers were away from the base, and instead of quashing American morale, the attack inflamed the nation. President Roosevelt declared to Congress the following day that the seventh of December was "a date which will live in infamy," and the U.S. declared war on Japan, and subsequently on Germany and Italy. And while Yamamoto, who had studied English at Harvard and served as a naval attaché in Washington, did not think much of the American Navy, he was aware of the strength of American industry, and after completing the raid reportedly acknowledged that all he had done was "awaken a sleeping giant and fill him with terrible resolve."

The day Germany invaded Poland in 1939, Roosevelt had made George C. Marshall the Army chief of staff. A straightforward leader from Uniontown, Pennsylvania, Marshall had enrolled in Virginia Military Institute as a teenager, and after receiving his commission had served in the Philippines and, during the First World War, in France and become known for inspiring his subordinates. Marshall then became an aide to the legendary General John "Black Jack" Pershing. With the Second World War and his new assignment, Marshall now had to inspire the whole military. He oversaw the development of new weapons, the training of troops and the expansion of the U.S. armed forces from 200,000 in 1939 to 8 million at the height of the war. Churchill appropriately dubbed him the "organizer of victory." Marshall also looked for qualified top commanders. Dwight D. Eisenhower, the son of a pacifist mother, quickly caught his eye. Eisenhower, who had won a Distinguished Service Medal in World War I and had served as an aide to General Douglas MacArthur, was seen as someone with great potential. He became a brigadier general in September 1941 and a major general in March 1942. Marshall appointed him to the Army's War Plans Division in Washington and was so impressed by Ike's ability to persuade and get along with others that in June 1942 he made him commander of U.S. troops in Europe. We will learn more about Eisenhower, the indispensable man, in a subsequent chapter of our book.

The United States and Great Britain now set forth a pooling of their economic and military resources, with a cooperative command and strategy. It was the beginning of the Grand Alliance. At the start, as mentioned, the going was tough. A Japanese military tsunami swept through Asia, taking Indochina in mid-1940, Malaya and Hong Kong in December 1941, Singapore in February 1942 and Burma and the Philippines that May. While America's priority was Europe, there needed to be focus on the Pacific as well and, particularly after Pearl Harbor, there was a desire to quickly show the Japanese that America could strike at the heart of that nation. U.S. Army Air Forces lieutenant colonel James

The War in North Africa

In the photograph below, a U.S. Air Transport Command plane flies supplies to strategic battle zones in 1943. The pyramids tell us that this matériel is to be used in the North African campaign, one of the most crucial thrusts before D-Day and, then, the final Pacific fights. The North African battles—in Libya, Egypt, Morocco, Algeria and Tunisia—had commenced in 1940 and would not be resolved until May 1943. This was more of a British operation on the Allied side, with the Italians more involved on the Axis side, but once the Americans were in, beginning on May 11, 1942, with military assistance, and once the German Afrika Korps commander Erwin Rommel was dispatched by Berlin to aid the Italians, this became one of the war's principal foci. The battle was push-pull, which made Stalin happy enough as it distracted Berlin from the Eastern Front. But who would win? Rommel was brilliant, British general Bernard Montgomery was dogged. Also dogged were the smarties in London who, with their code-breaking, gained crucial intelligence that allowed the Allies to attack with confidence and ultimately carry the day. After Africa was won, Italy would follow, and Germany would be alone.

"Jimmy" Doolittle, who served Stateside during World War I, said, "Americans badly needed a morale boost," and just four months after the Japanese assault on Hawaii, his Doolittle Raiders took off from the aircraft carrier *Hornet* and flew 16 B-25 bombers to Tokyo, Yokohama, Kobe and Nagoya. They arrived in Tokyo just after an air raid drill, and Japanese fighters thought they were part of the drill and did not attack. While their bombing raids did minimal damage—they burned down a hospital—and avoided attacking the Imperial Palace for fear of stiffening Japanese resolve, the attack sent a message, and earned Doolittle a Congressional Medal of Honor.

Then, after deciphering Japanese messages, the Americans defeated the Japanese in the Battle of the Coral Sea in May 1942. Yamamoto felt he had to finish off the rest of the American fleet the following month at Midway, 1,200 miles northwest of Hawaii. But by breaking the Japanese Purple Code, the Americans under Admiral Chester Nimitz figured out the position of the Japanese, and on the morning of June 4, dozens of Douglas Dauntless dive-bombers and Douglas Devastator torpedo bombers surprised the carriers *Kaga* and *Akagi*. Piles of bombs and high-octane gasoline covered the ships' decks, and they were quickly ablaze. One sailor later described the damage to the *Akagi:* "Deck plates reeled upwards in grotesque configurations. Planes stood tail up, belching livid flames and jet-black smoke." In six hours of fighting, the Americans swept away Japan's naval superiority, taking out two more carriers, along with a heavy cruiser, 270 planes and 3,500 men, and with a loss of only one carrier, 130 planes and 100 men. The American wave started to wash across the sea. While slow at times, it was unstoppable as Yanks started the brutal island-to-island slog toward Tokyo.

H ITLER HAD LONG WANTED TO BE RID OF THE JEWS, SEEing them as the incarnation of evil, the carriers of communism, of liberalism, of modern ideas. According to the Nuremberg Race Laws, those who had even one Jewish grandparent were tainted. Interestingly, Hitler's paternal grandmother, Maria Anna Schicklgruber, is known to have worked for the Frankenberger family, wealthy residents in Graz. It has been discussed that the Frankenbergers may have been Jewish. Maria became pregnant at this time, and when her son, Alois, was registered he was listed as illegitimate, and the father's name was not entered. The Frankenbergers also paid a paternity allowance for Alois until he was 14. This has created the rumor that Alois's father was one of the family's sons, and if he was, as thought, Jewish, it would have made Hitler, in the eyes of the Nazis, a quarter Jewish, and thus under the Nuremberg Race Laws eligible for the concentration camps. Rumors of his ancestry swirled as Hitler started his rise to power in 1930, and Hitler had his *Schutzstaffel,* the SS, look into it.

The investigation concluded that the family Maria worked for was not Jewish. And while the chances that Hitler was a quarter Jewish are minimal, the possibility weighed heavily on him. A doctor who knew Hitler from the time of World War I said that Hitler "suffered all his life from painful doubts: did he or did he not have Jewish blood?" In 2010 a Belgian magazine reported on DNA tests carried out on more than three dozen of Hitler's relatives. The results indicate that the Führer may have had both Jewish and African ancestry, possessing a chromosome that is rare in Germany and Western Europe but is commonly found among Ashkenazic and Sephardic Jews, as well as Moroccan Berbers and others. This is certainly nothing more than a footnote to our book, but it is fascinating nonetheless.

Regardless of his roots, after taking power Hitler worked to expel the Jews from greater Germany, and placed increasing restrictions on them. The Nazis soon started segregating the Jews, moving them into their own ghettos. The first in Poland, in Piotrków Trybunalski, opened in October 1939. The Nazis ended up establishing some 1,000 ghettos in Poland and the Soviet Union alone, and occupants had to wear Jewish Stars or armbands and take part in forced labor. They could be killed on a whim. There were large ghettos in such cities as Minsk, Kraków, Lodz, Bialystok, Lublin and Vilna. Warsaw had Poland's largest, with a 10-foot-high wall topped by barbed wire that surrounded the 1.3-square-mile community of 400,000, its buildings packed with seven people to a room. Guards watched the ghettos. Schools were forbidden. Diseases like typhus killed thousands. Food was limited, and residents tried to smuggle in food, medicine and weapons. Adam Czerniaków, a Jewish chemical engineer who was chairman of the *Judenrat,* the Jewish Council in Warsaw, wrote in May 1941 of "children starving to death." Conditions were so dire that from 1940 to 1942, 83,000 people perished from starvation and disease.

In September 1939, Hitler promised to get rid of the Jews if he was provoked, and in 1941 the Nazis started to put into action their plan to simply exterminate them. In July, Göring instructed General Reinhard Heydrich, whom Hitler referred to as "the man with the iron heart" to "carry out all preparations with regard to . . . a general solution of the Jewish question in those territories of Europe which are under German influence." At a conference in Wannsee in January 1942, Heydrich chaired a gathering of 15 Nazi Party members that set out the "Final Solution to the Jewish Question": the systematic murder of the 11 million Jews living in Europe.

The Holocaust, along with the liberation of the concentration camps, is, of course, an important part of our book—but it is in thousands of other books as well. We cannot do that astonishing horror justice in this space. Neither can we gloss over it. Efficiency was the aim of the Nazis. *Einsatzgruppen* were mobile killing squads that followed the

The Leaders

We will speak in more depth two chapters further on of General Dwight D. Eisenhower, seen at top, in May 1944, reviewing troops shortly before the Normandy invasion, while British general Bernard Montgomery looks over Ike's shoulder (which Monty hated to do). As for the other generals on this page, we have three famously vainglorious men, all of whom knew that the camera was operative when these pictures were taken. Let us hasten to add, and not in any pandering way but because we believe it: These brave men all were great, when greatness mattered to them and their nations. Bad guy first: At top right we have Field Marshal Erwin Rommel in a rare color photograph from 1942, when his Afrika Korps was moving forward. Above: Lieutenant General George S. Patton, soon to be promoted even further, in Africa in 1943. Right: Monty, whose British Eighth Army faced off with Rommel's troops. Ike had to wrestle Patton and Montgomery to the mat—in his studied but firm way—in order to keep control of the European offensive and allow Operation Overlord and D-Day to succeed.

army and slaughtered millions of Jews and others, shoving their bodies into mass graves. The Nazis soon realized that machine-gunning people was a waste of resources. So was stuffing people into hermetically sealed vans and pumping the interiors full of carbon monoxide. They needed a quicker, cheaper solution. They had already been using poison gas in their euthanasia program to eliminate tens of thousands of the mentally and physically handicapped, "the unworthy of life" at gassing installations in Bernburg, Brandenburg, Grafeneck, Hadamar, Hartheim and Sonnenstein. Now they decided to adapt it for larger-scale killing, first trying out Zyklon B, a gas used for fumigation, on Soviet prisoners in September 1941. And then it was simply a matter of rounding up and shipping people to camps.

Adolf Eichmann ran the Central Office for Jewish Emigration. He made sure the trains ran smoothly and cattle cars packed with human cargo moved nonstop to the camps. The killing centers were based in Poland, which had 3 million Jews before the war and not more than 100,000 after. Some were clearly charnel houses, remembered now with such ghastly names as Buchenwald, Dachau and Treblinka. At its height, Auschwitz gassed thousands of people a day, killing nearly a million Jews and more than 100,000 Poles, Roma, Russians and others by the end of the war. By that time, there were more than 20,000 concentration, slave labor, transit and prison camps in occupied Europe.

At the camps, guards immediately separated families, directing some to the right and some to the left. The young, the old, the handicapped, the sick and pregnant women were generally sent directly to the gas chambers. There they were told to strip for disinfecting showers to get rid of lice. As camp guards beat, whipped and stabbed them, they were herded into large rooms, and told to lift their arms. That way camp officials could pack more in at one time, and they would die faster when the gas pellets dropped in. Prisoners then pulled out the bodies, removed gold fillings, shaved off hair and sent the corpses to the crematoria or out to mass graves. Those who were not killed right away endured slow death in factories or in quarries at camps like Flossenbürg, Mauthausen, Natzweiler-Struthof and Gross-Rosen, where they cut stones for Nazi buildings. Work was hard, and they could be tortured, shot or bludgeoned to death for no reason. The crowded barracks lacked heating and were rife with disease. Food was limited. Heinrich Himmler, head of the SS and the second most powerful person in the Third Reich, was an agricultural graduate and a former poultry farmer. He established the Germans' first concentration camp, at Dachau, and was determined to find an inexpensive diet for inmates, similar to those given to Egyptian and Roman slaves. Some victims ended up in the clutches of physicians like Auschwitz's SS physician Josef Mengele. Called *Todesengel*, the Angel of Death, as well as *Der Weisse*

Raining Bombs on Germany

As we have learned, Churchill was quick to respond to the Nazi bombing of England with air raids on Berlin, beginning in 1940; obviously the United States joined in the effort after entering the war, and by early 1945 the German capital would have been hit more than 300 times. It needs to be noted just how brutal the Allied air campaign could be. In Hamburg in 1943, a huge firestorm was caused by incendiary bombs. Two years later, 1,300 British and American bombers attacked the medieval city of Dresden in two waves, again employing incendiary devices, again in hopes of starting widespread fires. An estimated 35,000 civilians were killed, many of them burned to death or suffocated by the fumes as they hid in basements. On the opposite page, circa 1942, a woman in Berlin wears a gas mask as she pushes a baby carriage through the streets after an Allied raid. Left: On June 11, 1943, wavy light trails are seen against the smoke caused by incendiary bombs that have been rained upon Düsseldorf by Britain's Royal Air Force.

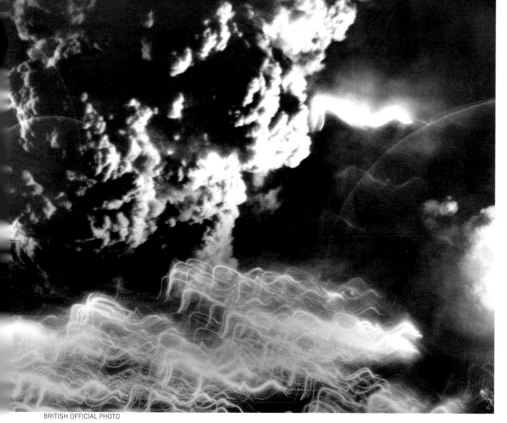

BRITISH OFFICIAL PHOTO

Engel, the White Angel, Mengele carried out pseudoscientific experiments in the hope of finding a way to increase German fertility rates. Overseeing a staff of some 30 physicians, he took a perverted interest in dwarfs, twins and people with two different eye colors, and wanted to study what happened when he amputated prisoners' limbs, froze people to death, locked them in pressure chambers or injected them with assorted drugs.

Between the camps, mobile killing squads and other methods, the Nazis systematically took the lives of 11 million men, women and children. Six million were Jews, and the rest were Roma, political prisoners, homosexuals, priests and nuns, the mentally and physically handicapped, Jehovah's Witnesses, Freemasons and others. Average Germans also knew what was going on, for when the British bombed them it was said they were being bombed because of the treatment of the Jews.

T
HE NAZIS WERE NOT ALONE IN THEIR ATROCITIES. THE Japanese indiscriminately slaughtered Chinese, Filipinos, Koreans, Indochinese and westerners, killing millions in their path. The Imperial Army unleashed anthrax, cholera and bubonic plague on its enemies. During a six-week orgy of rape and murder in Nanjing, China, Japanese soldiers killed 200,000 people. They pressed as many as 200,000 Korean and Chinese women—along with captured Dutch and Australians—into a prostitution corps euphemistically called "Comfort Women" to service their soldiers. Military units like the infamous Unit 731, which Hirohito established and which had a staff of 10,000, tested biological weapons on Chinese, Korean and Mongolian victims, as well as captured Russian soldiers and American aircrews. They vivisected the living and buried people alive.

Many Allies, too, behaved horribly in the war; people

do terrible things in war. But in June 1944, D-Day was seen as a righteous assault by most people in what we call the free world. These recounted incidents are a few of the reasons why.

IN JULY 1942 HITLER'S ARMIES ATTACKED STALINGRAD, and started a bitter siege of that town. Stalin had named the city on the Volga River for himself in 1925, and the Luftwaffe's incendiary bombs consumed the wooden buildings of this large industrial center. Stalin forbade people from escaping, ordering, *"Ni shagu nazad!"* (Not a step backwards!). Fighting proved so intense that during the battle the life span of the average private was just 24 hours. This was some of the worst block-by-block, hand-to-hand fighting of the war, with one defender recalling, "Our principle was to grab hold of the enemy and not let go; to hold him very

Into Italy

After the defeat of the Axis in North Africa, there was, as will be detailed in our chapter on Operation Overlord, beginning on page 58, much debate among Allied leaders about what to do next, with Winston Churchill in particular wanting to have a go at Italy. The measured Italian invasion, when it came in the summer of 1943, was twofold: first, a July attack on Axis forces on the island of Sicily (code name Operation Husky), followed by a three-pronged sweep onto the mainland at Salerno, Calabria and Taranto, beginning on September 3. Although Mussolini was deposed by King Victor Emmanuel III on July 25 and Italy seemed to be in chaos, none of this went easily for the Allies as many Axis troops were able to escape Sicily during a month of fighting there and then continue the battle on the mainland. (In fact, there would still be fighting in Italy after Paris had been liberated and Berlin taken.) Opposite: On August 9, sympathetic Sicilians look on as Private Roy Humphrey of Toledo, Ohio, is given blood plasma while being tended to by Private First Class Harvey White of Minneapolis. Below: On September 12, as the Germans are mounting a furious counterattack on the mainland, a member of General Montgomery's 9th Battalion, Royal Fusiliers, takes aim from the window of a ruined house.

The War Before '44

The Big Three in Tehran

This was the first of two conferences to feature Stalin, Roosevelt and Churchill; the second would be held near the city of Yalta, on the shores of the Black Sea, in February 1945, not long before FDR's death. At the Tehran meeting, code-named Eureka and carried out amid extraordinary security, the tone was generally

close—as you'd hold a loved one." Another wrote, "I wanted only one thing—to kill. You know how it looks when you squeeze a tomato and juice comes out? Well, it looked like that when I stabbed them. Blood everywhere. Every step in Stalingrad meant death. Death was in our pockets. Death was walking with us." Winter soon descended, and the Germans could not get sufficient food or ammunition. Hitler ordered General Friedrich Paulus to "stand and fight," but his troops were exhausted, and on January 31, 1943, he, two dozen other generals and 91,000 men surrendered. The battle had resulted in 800,000 dead Axis fighters, with losses of 1.1 million for the Soviets. It halted the Nazi advance, and it was after this fight that Hitler acknowledged that "the God of War has gone over to the other side."

The Germans were on the run. In January 1943, Roosevelt and Churchill met in Casablanca to plan their strategies. Stalin was invited, but he did not attend, and while figuring out the eventual invasion of France, they decided to conquer Sicily and mainland Italy in order to knock Mussolini out of the war. They also made plans for getting Japan out of New Guinea, opening up supply lines in Japanese-occupied Burma and bombing Germany. Nuclear bomb research was broached, as well as a need for an "unconditional surrender" by Germany, Japan and Italy. This was something that, Roosevelt insisted, did not mean the destruction of civilians of the Axis powers, only "the destruction of the philosophies in those countries which are based on conquest and the subjugation of other people." He was quite adamant about this, and did not want a repeat of the situation that followed World War I, where the losing side claimed that its nation had been, as he put it, "stabbed in the back."

In November and December of 1943, Stalin joined Roosevelt and Churchill in Tehran. These leaders coordinated their strategy against Germany and Japan, and discussed Operation Overlord, the plan for the invasion of France. They then talked about the postwar fate of Germany and eastern Europe and broached the question of the possible partition of Germany. Roosevelt also described for Stalin his vision of a United Nations dominated by the United States, Britain, China and the Soviet Union—a group that could effectively and powerfully "deal immediately with any threat to the peace and any sudden emergency which requires action."

If the end was in sight for these men and others, the war was still not ended. Operation Overlord seemed promising but daunting. Nineteen forty-four—and indeed '45—awaited the Allies, and the world.

DANIEL S. LEVY WROTE FOR LIFE BOOKS ON THE ZAPRUDER FILM IN 2013'S *THE DAY KENNEDY DIED: 50 YEARS LATER* LIFE *REMEMBERS THE MAN AND THE MOMENT.*

optimistic, tempered by the realization that many battles remained to be fought and many lives would be lost. As we will learn more fully in our chapter on Operation Overlord, Roosevelt and Stalin essentially carried the day over Churchill in committing the Allies to the establishment of a second European front with an attack by the western Allies to be launched from England—the attack that would become D-Day. Ancillary business included discussions of Iran's sovereignty, operations in Yugoslavia, the fight against Japan (Stalin said the Soviets might join in) and preliminary imaginings of what the postwar world might look like.

The World Stage—1944

The first so-called world war eventuated largely in Europe. The second indeed encompassed action all over the globe (Japan even taking two Alaskan islands). In '44, the Allies, after years of fighting uphill, had finally reached "the point of balance."

By John Keegan

WHAT HAD BEGUN IN SEPTEMBER 1939 AS A LOCAL north European conflict between Germany and Poland had swelled by January 1944 into a war that embraced four of the world's seven continents, all of its oceans and most of its states.

Millions had already died, and millions more were soon to die, the majority in the great land, air and sea offensives that the United States, the Soviet Union and the British Empire were poised to deliver against the conquered and occupied territories dominated by Germany and Japan.

The opponents of Germany and Japan had recovered from the shock of their enemies' opening successes, had built vast war industries, armies, navies and air forces and had already reoccupied parts of the territory lost in the early years. Most, however, remained in enemy hands.

In Asia the perimeter of the Japanese area of conquest still enclosed a majority of the islands of the western Pacific, the Dutch East Indies, Burma, Malaya and coastland China. In Europe the German front line still ran deep inside Russia, while all continental European states, except Switzerland, Sweden, Spain and Portugal, were either under German occupation or under governments allied to Germany. Only in Italy, which had changed sides in 1943, did the Western Allies, Britain and America have a foothold inside Hitler's Fortress Europe.

Yet the point of balance had been reached and was soon to tip sharply in the Allies' favor. Except in China, where the Japanese would win huge areas of rich agricultural land during 1944 in the so-called rice offensives mounted to feed the home population, the dictatorships had lost the power to stage large-scale attacks.

In March, the Japanese would attempt an invasion of

On African Beachheads; in Berlin Airspace

Previous pages: Down the ramp, through the surf and up the beach dash Royal British Marines from a U.S. Coast Guard–manned landing craft during final amphibious assault maneuvers on the coast of North Africa in 1944. Finally, the Allies are able to put one front—and one continent—behind them. Left: In a U.S. Army Air Forces photograph made on March 8, 1944, a Boeing B-17 Flying Fortress of the U.S. Eighth Air Force passes over an aircraft-equipment manufacturing plant at Erkner, about 15 miles southeast of the center of Berlin, during an air raid. The military would release such photographs domestically to prove the war's progress, this one accompanied by a caption reading in part: "Smoke clouds below attest the damage inflicted." The Flying Fortress, which had been developed in the 1930s, was an important part of the Allied air arsenal. It was usually deployed in daylight salvos, as here, against Nazi industrial and military targets. It partnered in the Combined Bomber Offensive with British night raiders. The goal of the offensive in 1944 was to secure air superiority over western Europe in anticipation of Operation Overlord, the invasion of France.

The World Stage—1944

India from Burma, but it was defeated by the heroic defense of the cities of Kohima and Imphal by the Fourteenth Army, composed of British and Indian troops. In the Pacific islands and the East Indies archipelago, the Japanese were everywhere on the defensive, against widespread attacks by the U.S. Army, Navy and Marine Corps and the forces of Australia and New Zealand.

Germany also had lost its capacity to threaten the survival of its opponents. At sea the U-boats had been defeated.

On land the Red Army was on the offensive, while in Italy the Americans and British were pushing relentlessly up the peninsula.

In the air battle Hitler placed much hope in the pilotless weapons he was about to deploy against Britain's home islands. The Luftwaffe, however, had been reduced to a home defense force, as the strength of the American and British strategic bomber forces grew to a point at which they could fly devastating thousand-bomber raids against cities

across the length and breadth of Germany by day and night.

Britain and America had agreed at the Trident Conference, in May 1943, to launch a cross-Channel invasion in 1944. On June 6 an armada of 4,000 ships, overflown by 13,000 aircraft, landed 180,000 troops on beaches in Normandy. The Germans, taken by surprise, counterattacked, but by June 12 the bridgeheads had been consolidated and the invaders began to wear down the enemy's resistance. On July 25 the Americans broke out, and on August 20 they

and the British encircled the German army at the town of Falaise. The survivors fled across the Seine with the Allies in close pursuit. Paris was liberated on August 25, Brussels on September 3. On August 15 a Franco-American force landed in the south of France. By October the Germans were defending their own western frontier.

In the east the Red Army had opened a major offensive, promised to the Western Allies, on June 22, the third anniversary of Hitler's attack on Russia. It resulted in the

Cities in Ruins

These two scenes from Cologne, Germany, in 1944—of the main railway station and a roofless church during Mass—indicate the effectiveness of the Allies' Combined Bomber Offensive. The noted historian and war correspondent Alan Moorehead later described moving through these cities with British forces as the war neared its end: "The Germany in which we found ourselves traveling . . . presented a scene that was almost beyond human comprehension. Her capital was lost and almost razed, and [there was] nothing to give that ash-heap significance beyond a name, a history and the presence of a lunatic who was about to make his last gesture to a colossal vanity—his death. Around us 50 great cities lay in ruins . . . Many [of them] had no electric light or power or gas or running water, and no coherent system of government. Like ants in an ant heap the people scurried over the ruins diving furtively into cellars in search of loot. Everyone was on the move, and there was a frantic, antlike quality about their activity. Life was sordid, aimless, leading nowhere." Because cities, as opposed to rural towns, were the principal targets of the bombers, there were evacuees throughout the land: "Every house in every unbombed village was stacked to the roof with city refugees living on soup and potatoes."

The World Stage—1944

destruction of Army Group Center and led to an advance to Warsaw, where on August 1 the Polish Home Army rose in revolt against German occupation. Stalin cynically allowed the Germans to defeat the Warsaw uprising before liberating the rest of Poland, in which he installed a puppet Communist regime.

The disasters of June in the West and East triggered a military revolt in Germany. On July 20 a bomb placed by the leader of the conspiracy exploded under Hitler's conference table. He survived and took terrible reprisals. The failure of the bomb plot actually reinforced his power over his country, which remained absolute, even as his European empire crumbled. In September both Finland and Bulgaria made peace with Russia, Romania fell to the Red Army, and German troops evacuated Greece and Yugoslavia. By

Progress in Italy

To be clear: Not every American or British foot soldier was, in late May and early June of 1944, massing in southern England in anticipation of the Operation Overlord assault (which was already, just then, delayed because of the lack of sufficient numbers of landing craft). The U.S. Army 3rd infantry and 1st Armored Divisions, for instance, took Cisterna in Italy (and took these soldiers, opposite, prisoner on May 26) after fierce fighting against elite German units. Below: Days later, an American soldier runs for cover while under fire from the Germans at Nemi Castle during the battle for Rome. The point to be made: Even before D-Day, the Allies were intent on keeping the pressure on, squeezing the Reich and building momentum. The Nazis were forced to make decisions. Send the best-armed and most-talented forces east to battle the Soviets, south to try to hold Italy or into France or Norway in anticipation of whatever in the world was brewing in England? Balance between the Axis and the Allies had finally been achieved. If the field was now level, the second half of 1944 would certainly be tipped once more—one way or the other.

December most of Germany's conquests from 1939 to 1942 had been liberated, and the Allies were poised to invade Germany itself.

In the Pacific the Japanese home islands were not yet under threat. United States forces possessed no base from which they could be struck. On the two major oceanic fronts, however—General MacArthur's in the Southwest Pacific, Admiral Nimitz's in the Central Pacific—huge naval, ground and air forces were preparing to advance. MacArthur's initial aim was to expel the enemy from the island of New Guinea and neutralize the great Japanese base at Rabaul, in the Solomon Islands. Both aims were achieved, at remarkably little cost, by June.

Meanwhile in the Central Pacific, Nimitz's vast fleet of aircraft carriers began a drive through the islands, designed to land amphibious forces and seize bases from which Japan could be attacked by strategic bombers. In January the offensive began with the capture of the Marshall Islands. Step-by-step advances led to the seizure of important footholds in the Marianas, including Saipan, from which the new B-29 bomber could hit Japan.

The offensive provoked Japan into a counteroffensive that resulted in the decisive battle of the Philippine Sea, June 19 and 20. Admiral Ozawa, with most of Japan's surviving

The Fall of Rome

Obviously the great cities are, in a war, the great prizes—not just another stepping stone, but symbols of a people, a culture, a nation. When Paris fell to the Germans on June 14, 1940, leaders in London (and in Washington and in Berlin) knew what that meant. And so, with the Allies pressing back in 1944, even before ticking off the German cities leading to Berlin, there were two prominent national capitals to be reclaimed from the Nazis: Rome and Paris. The latter would require D-Day, but the former was a target of this Italian offensive, launched earlier. We say "the fall of Rome" rather than "the liberation of Rome" because, remember, Italy and Mussolini's Fascists were all-in with the Axis from the get-go; there was no conquest or even coercion, except for pressure by the dictator, who for many years was very popular. Il Duce had no influence by the time the Allies were pressuring Rome in the first half of 1944; he had been gone from power for more than half a year by then, and would be executed within months, as we will see on the pages immediately following. Allied landings at Anzio, 35 miles south of Rome, had been bottled up by the Germans, and it took four major offensives between January and May of 1944 to break the enemy line and allow the Fifth and Eighth Armies to rush toward the capital. Since Germany and Italy had been friends, Rome was an "open city," with no defenses suitable for warfare. After all of the trouble everywhere in Italy and Sicily, the entrance of American troops on June 4, only two days before the launch of Operation Overlord to the northeast, was a waltz. It is pictured here with the Colosseum as a backdrop.

carriers and naval aircraft, was devastated by Admiral Spruance's Fifth Fleet. Ozawa lost three carriers and, in the "Great Marianas Turkey Shoot," almost 400 irreplaceable aircraft and their crews. After the capture of the Marianas and the victory of the Philippine Sea, the defeat of Japan was inevitable.

Success in the Central Pacific prompted President Roosevelt to approve General MacArthur's plan for the recapture of the Philippines. The landings began on the island of Leyte on October 20. In response the Japanese decided to concentrate their fleets and challenge the Americans to a climactic sea battle. Four major surface

engagements, largely fought in the narrow waters of the Philippine archipelago, resulted in the loss of four Japanese carriers, three battleships, 10 cruisers and 500 aircraft. American losses were light. After these Leyte battles Japan had no further offensive power. Its home islands now came under attack from B-29 bombers based in the Marianas, the first of which was flown on November 24.

By December 1, it seemed that both Germany and Japan trembled on the brink of defeat. Desperation, however, was to draw from each the power to inflict unexpected loss on their opponents. On December 16, Hitler launched a surprise offensive against the Americans in the Ardennes, the

Battle of the Bulge, which was defeated by the Allies with difficulty. In the Pacific the Japanese prepared to fight a last-ditch defense of the Philippines and on the islands of Iwo Jima and Okinawa.

The sufferings of noncombatants increased. Holland, isolated by the Anglo-American advance to the German frontier, suffered a terrible "hunger winter." London continued to flinch under bombardments by V-2 rockets. Normal life in Greece, the Balkans and Eastern Europe was interrupted by civil war and the depredations of occupying armies. The cities of Germany quivered under the relentless assault of the Anglo-American air forces. In the concentration camps the business of systematic cruelty and extermination ground on. The year of 1944 was a terrible 12 months, which the approach of victory in 1945 did little to alleviate. Peace would be no consolation to those who suffered and died in the final agonies of the conflict.

SIR JOHN KEEGAN WAS KNIGHTED IN 2000 FOR HIS ACHIEVEMENTS IN MILITARY HISTORY. HE WROTE SOME 20 BOOKS, OF WHICH *THE FACE OF BATTLE* IS PERHAPS THE BEST KNOWN, AND FOR MORE THAN 25 YEARS WAS A SENIOR LECTURER AT THE ROYAL MILITARY ACADEMY SANDHURST. BEFORE HIS DEATH, IN 2012, HE WROTE THIS ESSAY FOR LIFE.

CARL MYDANS

BRUNI FOTOGRAFICO

The Emphatic End of Mussolini

At left we see Romans glorying in the Allied entrance into their city in 1944, as if none of them had ever sided with the Fascists. This happens in every war—which way is the wind blowing?—and certainly many Italians came to different conclusions about the rightness or wrongness of the Axis between, say, 1938 and 1944. Mussolini, of course, could not—and would not—change his mind. After being deposed in 1943, he was, in some quarters, a wanted man, and certainly his fate became much more perilous after the Allies moved in. Nevertheless, he lived on—for a while. He and his latest mistress, Clara Petacci, were headed for Switzerland in April 1945, whence they hoped to escape by air to Spain with several other Fascists (technically, members of the Italian Social Republic). The lot of them were apprehended by Italian communists. They were brought to Mezzegra and, on April 28, shot to death. The following day, their bodies were transported south by van to Milan, where they were deposited on the plaza, then hung up on meat hooks from the roof of an Esso gas station. That is Mussolini on the far right, above, and Petacci next to him, and then two of their fellow travelers. The bodies were spat at and stoned by the Italians below, who dared to hope that this was the end of something. Something that, certainly, many of them had once supported but would never again admit to having supported.

Ike: The Indispensable Man

He was in no way as grand as some of his Allied associates—Patton, Montgomery. He was measured and purposeful. He was also strong and decisive. He was a latter-day Washington.

By Robert Sullivan

AN OFTEN-NOTED HISTORICAL IRONY IS THAT THE AXIS ultimately suffered—fatally—because Albert Einstein and other great Jewish thinkers fled Nazi Germany for the free world in the years before the war. By chance, the Third Reich had lost out much earlier when, in 1741, the Eisenhauer family (changed to Eisenhower) emigrated from Germany to Bethel Township, Pennsylvania, later continuing on to Kansas. David Dwight Eisenhower (the first and middle names would be reversed) was born in Denison, Texas, in 1890, and two years later his family returned to Kansas—to Abilene—with their last $24. Dwight's father, David, worked as a mechanic at a creamery, and forged a living for the family. One day, a younger brother of Dwight's lost an eye in an accident. Dwight resolved to be more protective of others.

There was a man named Bob Davis who camped along the Smoky Hill River. Ike took to him and learned ruggedness: hunting, fishing, exploring. He also learned to play cards and get along well. At home, he was schooled in firm discipline and Bible study. Later in life he joined the Presbyterian Church and professed himself "one of the most deeply religious men I know."

He was not boisterous but willful. After he badly injured his leg in high school, a doctor urged amputation, but the boy refused it. His mother was what can fairly be termed a pacifist—she felt war "rather wicked"—and yet it was her collection of books that spurred Dwight's interest in military history. A smart boy, he sought Annapolis or West Point and was accepted into the Army military academy, disappointing his mother, who nonetheless let him go.

Beginning in 1911, he enjoyed many pursuits on the campus above the Hudson (he and Omar Bradley were teammates on the baseball team, and in football he once tackled Jim Thorpe) but was not a star student. He graduated in 1915 with a group of young men known since as "the class the stars fell on," as no fewer than 59 of them would become Army generals. This happened, of course, because of the advent of two world wars. Generals would be needed, and it was good for the nation that the Class of '15 was a class of substance.

Stationed in Texas, Ike met Mamie Geneva Doud. They were to be married in November 1916, but this was hastened to July because it became clear the United States was about to enter World War I. Lieutenant Eisenhower served Stateside during that conflict, a fact that was later derided by men such as British general Bernard Montgomery, who had led soldiers in conflict during the Great War.

Such denigration fell on deaf ears, because by the time Eisenhower stepped into the role for which he was predestined, by dint of courage and character, it was clear to all that he was the right leader at the right time. The historian James Thomas Flexner has called George Washington "the indispensable man" of the American Revolution—and, indeed, of his epoch. Washington was stalwart, he was forceful, he could inspire. There were firebrands around him, men who would fall into conflict with one another when he was absent. Yet Washington was a man of not only strength but equilibrium: the very person needed at a critical moment. The nascent nation placed its bet with that man, thinking that if anyone could succeed, Washington might be the one. Abraham Lincoln would be another such man.

In World War II, when General George C. Marshall, chief of staff, looked at his ranks, there was Dwight David Eisenhower. If anyone could do this thing, Ike could.

The Right Stuff

It is cliché to say that such as Eisenhower emerged in the first half of the 20th century from the heartland instilled with what was then coming to be known as "American values": seriousness of purpose, a certain boldness, a quiet ambition, a resolve formed by periods of family poverty but also a sense of wanting to contribute to America. He was drawn to the military, and eventually to war. Left: the Eisenhower family in 1902. In the front row, left to right, are David Eisenhower, the father; Milton; and Ida Eisenhower, the mother. Behind, are Dwight, Edgar, Earl, Arthur and Roy. Opposite: Ike during his days coaching the Army football team, having already played there for two seasons.

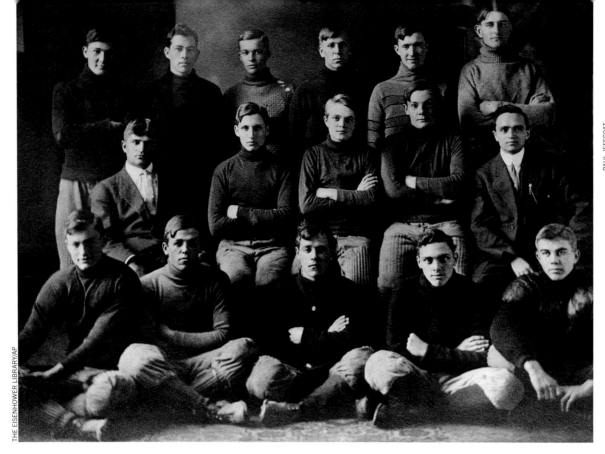

Americana

If the Eisenhower upbringing had been a little more exciting, it could have served as material for a Frank Capra movie. As it was, it formed a heroic American general. Good for us. Above, we have the Abilene (Kansas) High School football team of 1910, on which Ike played while a postgraduate student (red-shirting, a hundred years ago!) in preparation for West Point. He is in the back row, third from left. In the photograph at left are Ike and the former Mamie Doud in 1916, three days after their war-hastened wedding. Eisenhower still had hair, if not for long, and was sufficiently dashing that this photo looks like a still from *Downton Abbey.* At right is an Eisenhower reunion in Abilene in 1926. All the boys are doing well at this point. Roy (left) is a pharmacist in Junction City, Kansas; Arthur (second from left) is a Kansas City banker; Earl (next) is an electrical engineer; Edgar (standing beside his seated father) is a prosperous lawyer; Milton (next to his mother) is on leave from the consular service. Ike—well, "Dwight"—is at this juncture a major in the Army, and can be identified by his uniform. The family patriarch would die in 1942, the matriarch four years later. He would not see his son's glory; she would, if briefly. Neither would witness Ike's ascension to his nation's top office.

A Man of War

Looking back, it seems that there was no one on the planet capable of marshaling George S. Patton and Bernard Montgomery—no one except Ike. The marshaling of Montgomery certainly didn't come easy (it was tougher even than Ike's and George Marshall's dealings with Patton). The British general angled, more than once, for the top job in whatever would be the ultimate European assault. Request denied, and the usually decorous Eisenhower bothered to say, in effect, get him off my back. As for Patton (below, right, with Ike at the Palermo airport in Sicily on September 17, 1943): Well, he was an American general, and was required to obey orders. Ike did find a temperamental kinsman in his old West Point teammate Omar Bradley, who would be so crucial on D-Day, but still there was all this political maneuvering after Ike had been named Supreme Commander of the Allied Expeditionary Force (bottom, photographers attend the announcement in Ike's London office in 1944). Eisenhower and the Allies would prevail, of course, and in 1945, Ike takes the classic American hero's trip under a shower of ticker tape on New York City's Wall Street (right). Monty or Patton might have made more of the moment. Ike: He was surely happy enough.

A Man of Peace

With the war over, Ike assumed a natural post: Army chief of staff under FDR's successor, Harry S Truman. He was offered the job of president of Columbia University and accepted. Public service called him out of what looked like semiretirement, and he ran as a Republican in the 1952 presidential election. It was, as it had been with George Washington so long ago, almost an enthronement: He buried Adlai Stevenson in the general election, and would do so again four years later. (Opposite, center, is Ike with, from left, his wife, Mamie; Pat Nixon; and Richard M. Nixon, who has been nominated as his vice presidential running mate during the 1952 convention in Chicago.) The New Deal coalition of 20 years' standing was defeated, and Ike, despite the fact that many Americans now look back at the 1950s as a time of complacency, showed a New Look to the world. He supported (sponsored, even) the Iranian coup d'etat of 1953, and by brandishing his nuclear arsenal not only ended the Korean War with China but faced off against the salivating Soviet Union in the eventually escalating Cold War. Domestically—and this will surprise some readers—he initiated the Interstate Highway System, boosted NASA and sent federal troops to Little Rock, Arkansas, to enforce integration at Central High School, the first such executive order issued since Reconstruction. He signed separate civil rights bills in 1957 and 1960 to protect the right of African Americans and all others to vote. And then, having served his two terms—and having served his country in so many ways—he retired. He golfed, he fished. He never bragged about what he had done in World War II—he was an exemplar of that classic, anonymous D-Day soldier who, if he said he was there and had done this and that, perhaps hadn't been there at all. Below, left: Ike in retirement on his farm in Gettysburg, Pennsylvania, in June 1961. Below: His casket lies in state in the U.S. Capitol Building on March 30, 1969—by which time too many Americans had forgotten, or didn't properly regard and honor, what this great, indispensable man had meant to America and to the free world.

RALPH MORSE

ED CLARK

BURT GLINN/MAGNUM

Overlord:
The Drumbeat to D-Day

**Much was secret as the theoretical Operation Overlord was assembled
in flesh-and-blood terms in England. But this military enterprise was so big—the biggest
ever in history—that everyone from little kids to Hitler knew something was brewing.**

Overlord: The Drumbeat to D-Day

"A MERICAN INVADERS MASS IN ENGLAND" READ A HEAD-line in the May 15, 1944, issue of LIFE, and the caption continued: "The men from the United States, carrying bayoneted Springfield rifles, get going across England . . ."

What does this tell us? It tells us where we were and what we were headed for in that perilous spring season.

Daniel Levy has delineated for us what had come before in this titanic conflict known as World War II, and the late Sir John Keegan's essay on 1944 helps us understand all that was going on, everywhere, during that crucial year; Douglas Brinkley will shortly deliver us to the heart of "the longest day." Before we get there, let us look inside the buildup, listen to the drumbeat.

The date of that issue of LIFE—May 15, 1944—indicates beyond any doubt that D-Day, while an extraordinary surprise in its execution, was not any kind of surprise to the Allied and Axis military leaders: Americans were massing in England with purpose. It had been almost precisely four years since the last boats had pushed off the beach at Dunkirk, France, heading for home with the dead and wounded, and it seemed clear to all that another crossing of the English Channel, in the assertive direction, was to be attempted. If there was no hiding that from LIFE, there was certainly no reason to try to hide the fact from the enemy. There would be feints, as Brinkley will point out, and the

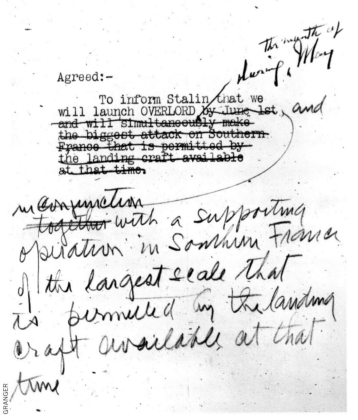

Putting Things in Place

On the pages immediately previous: In April 1944, English children, watched over by an American guard from Army Service Forces, enjoy the show from a cliffside fence as U.S. troops practice landings along Slapton Sands in Devon in southwestern England. On these pages, we see evidence of preparations intellectual and physical, on our side and theirs. At the Tehran Conference in November 1943, which certainly had its tensions, the crucial agreement between Roosevelt, Churchill and Stalin was that the Western Front of the European war be established (or at least attempted) through the execution of Operation Overlord. Such a serious declaration of will needed confirmation in writing (left, a memorandum issued on November 30). Above, top: If the so-called Big Three were their nations' leaders, then a military Big Two of Operation Overlord were Supreme Allied Commander General Dwight D. Eisenhower (holding binoculars) and Air Chief Marshal Sir Arthur Tedder (as if from central casting, with pipe in mouth)—here reviewing an American armored unit taking part in preinvasion maneuvers "somewhere in England." Bottom: German soldiers on alert at their fortified bunker somewhere along the Atlantic Wall defenses in Normandy in April 1944. Opposite: On April 29, Churchill himself and Eisenhower reviewed this rehearsal drop of U.S. paratroopers. During his two-day visit to the staging area, Churchill took target practice with a machine gun and a .30 carbine and, it was said, scored a number of hits.

Overlord: The Drumbeat to D-Day

BOB LANDRY

RALPH MORSE

Calm Before a Storm

Left: This picture ran in the May 15, 1944, issue of LIFE, and the caption pointed out that the men were drilling in England "under the flags of their country and their regiment"—so as to the work that was being done, there were no secrets. In their downtime, the men who were about to risk their lives enjoyed life as they could. In the photograph at left, bottom, an American soldier and his English girlfriend relish a quiet moment in Hyde Park on a lovely day in May. The lake in that vast London park, called the Serpentine, was employed by the Allies for practice in wading ashore, rifles held high. Right: A U.S. soldier pitches in at jump rope in a village in the south of England. The vehicles lining the street and the equipment in them are all destined for shipment to France, as is this serviceman.

best of them would succeed in throwing the Nazis off. But Hitler knew his foe was coming, if not when or where.

Brinkley will explain as well the vagaries of the weather, the debates over a launch date and the reasons the Germans guessed wrong about Normandy. He will also explain the nomenclature, but for now it is important only to know this: It wasn't "D-Day" until it commenced. Before that it was known by a code name, the aforementioned Operation Overlord, a plan born from an agreement between Roosevelt, Churchill and Stalin that a "second front" was needed in the European war, even though, in 1942 and '43, there was not yet sufficient Allied might or momentum to establish one.

By 1944 there was, it was desperately hoped, sufficient strength, and the effort to make good on Churchill's 1940

pledge—the liberation of France—began to move forward materially as well as strategically.

The 1942 announcement of an "understanding" among the Allies that a second front was a critical aim caused Hitler to fortify for an invasion. This he did. Beachheads became fortresses, hidden and unhidden bunkers were constructed by the score. Munitions were moved into place.

Churchill in particular was wary as plans were made. A great British defeat and a personal one (he was the First Lord of the Admiralty) during World War I had been the attempt to control the sea route from Europe to Russia with a direct naval invasion on the Turkish peninsula of Gallipoli—an attack that ended in disaster and massive British death. Now he lobbied for insurgency, special-ops work, subterfuge. In fact, he and his staff floated a course of action that would

see the Allies sweep south across the Mediterranean Sea and invade via Vienna, pummeling Italy before taking on the mightier Germans: "Why stick your head in the alligator's mouth at Brest, when you can go to the Mediterranean and rip his soft underbelly?" But the Americans, being Americans, felt a direct, shorter route from a well-fortified base to be built in Britain was best, and by this point the Americans were largely in charge. How much in charge? General George Marshall derided any potential excursions into the Mediterranean as "periphery-picking" that could wind up being a "suction pump" on manpower, resources and energy. He felt a big, big battle was coming, one way or the other—a battle that might decide the war—and he wanted to engage it. He made rumbling noises that if the British didn't come around on this, the United States might

The Clock Ticks

In early June of 1944, U.S. troops and vehicles are poured into the open mouths of landing ships in the (usually) small fishing town of Brixham, in Devon, England. It's funny in a way: After four years of war, Britain largely took the D-Day preparations in stride. Here by the water, boats are being loaded for war, while elsewhere in Brixham, laundry is hung in the garden to dry on this fine day.

DAVID E. SCHERMAN

shift its focus to the Pacific. The British pointed out that a cross-Channel invasion in 1943 was impossibly hazardous, as Allied transport ships were still being sunk in the North Atlantic and there just wouldn't be enough artillery and landing craft delivered from America to counter the 136 German divisions in France and the Low Countries (an extra 44 in reserve). Okay, said the United States, not in '43. But soon.

Two notions were floated: Operation Sledgehammer, which in fact was originally thought of as early as 1942, and the larger Operation Roundup, which evolved into Operation Overlord and would eventually become D-Day. The plan was articulated with optimism and eventual prescience in a report by the Allied Chiefs of Staff at a conference in Quebec City, Canada, in August 1943: "This operation will be the primary United States and British ground and air effort against the Axis of Europe . . . Following the establishment of strong Allied forces in France, operations designed to strike at the heart of Germany and to destroy her military forces will be undertaken . . . We have approved the outline plan for Operation Overlord." Still, even at the tense first summit of the Big Three—Roosevelt, Stalin, Churchill—in Tehran, in late November 1943, Churchill wondered about the Mediterranean. More action in Italy, he posited, maybe Greece. Stalin interjected at this point: The Nazis were thick on his own soil, and piddling matters would do little to change the German focus. "If we are here to discuss military matters," he said, "then Russia's only

interest is in Overlord." Roosevelt, knowing his own and his generals' minds, was happy to hear this, and it was decided that an invasion would be launched no later than the following May. "I realized at Tehran for the first time," Churchill later wrote, "what a small nation we are. There I sat with the great Russian bear on one side of me, with paws outstretched, and on the other side sat the great American buffalo, and between the two sat the poor little English donkey who was the only one, the only one of the three, who knew the right way home."

That was surely how he felt in that time, at that place. Certainly he was not dismayed by how things turned out.

The North African campaign against Erwin Rommel had turned into an arduous tug-of-war, and though the Allies would prevail, this slowed the buildup in Britain. But with North Africa having finally been settled, Italy having been taken out of the equation after the invasion of Sicily (38 days to capture an island about the size of Vermont!) and

The Clock Ticks On

Left: The landing ships are berthed in this small English harbor as American soldiers endeavor to keep fit in the hours leading up to the launch of Overlord. Right: Free French ambulance drivers (you can tell by the cross of Lorraine on their helmets) are in England and ready to go. Below: With their assault craft providing a subtle but significant backdrop, these members of the first wave receive a blessing from an Army chaplain. There are a mere hundred or so people pictured on these two pages, but they had tens of thousands of others going into France from England with them. Their thoughts and prayers as the clock ticked on were sometimes recorded, as we have seen in our texts, but most often they can only be imagined.

the war distilling to simple matters (simple to understand, if not to overcome), even LIFE was chronicling the "American invaders" massing in England. Everyone knew something was coming. Roosevelt, forthrightly, warned what it meant in his 1943 Christmas message: "The war is now reaching the stage when we shall have to look forward to large casualty lists—dead, wounded and missing. War entails just that. There is no easy road to victory. And the end is not yet in sight."

As to the massing: Eisenhower had been picked as Supreme Commander of the Allied Expeditionary Force, and in January 1944, he met with three Englishmen who would serve directly under him (the first of them chafingly): General Bernard Montgomery (handling ground forces), Admiral Bertram Ramsay and Air Chief Marshal Trafford Leigh-Mallory. What they discussed: Three million Allied military men and women would assemble in England in the coming months. A fleet of more than 5,000 vessels would be built or delivered there, and because the Germans held the nearby ports, artificial harbors called Mulberries, which could be transported across the Channel in parts and then reassembled off the French shore, would be built. All of this was in support of the invasion: nine divisions comprising more than 100,000 men landing along 50 miles of Normandy beaches in a single day. Hundreds of thousands of men would follow them in subsequent waves. The generals talked up the decoy targets—maybe Norway? Maybe Pas-de-Calais, which is the nearest point across the Channel?—decoys that Douglas Brinkley will help us understand in our book's next chapter. So too will he tell us of other matters that mattered greatly to the Allied leaders as they planned: clear skies for 12,000 aircraft (the planes would soften up enemy defenses and deliver paratroopers), the need of moonlight, a rising low tide at sunrise, calm-enough seas. No invasion on this scale in the history of man had ever been attempted, and Eisenhower and his colleagues knew it.

The Clock Continues

Opposite: In those first few days of June 1944, on board the attack transport USS *Samuel Chase,* named for a signatory of the Declaration of Independence, men confer over a model of Omaha Beach. Right: Eisenhower boosts the men of the 101st Airborne Division on June 5 (that very day, paratroopers are deployed: the beginning of the invasion). Below: General Montgomery seeks to inspire the men of the Second Army of the Allied Forces on the same day. What did Ike and Monty say? History tells us. Supreme Commander Eisenhower's D-Day exhortation: "Soldiers, sailors and airmen of the Allied Expeditionary Force, you are about to embark upon a great crusade, toward which we have striven these many months. The eyes of the world are upon you. The hopes and prayers of liberty-loving people everywhere march with you. In company with our brave allies and brothers in arms on other fronts, you will bring about the destruction of the German war machine, the elimination of Nazi tyranny over the oppressed peoples of Europe and security for ourselves in a free world.

"Your task will not be an easy one. Your enemy is well trained, well equipped and battle hardened. He will fight savagely.

"But this is the year 1944! Much has happened since the Nazi triumphs of 1940–41. The united nations have inflicted upon the Germans great defeats, in open battle, man to man. Our air offensive has seriously reduced their strength in the air and their capacity to wage war on the ground. Our home fronts have given us an overwhelming superiority in weapons and munitions of war and placed at our disposal great reserves of trained fighting men. The tide has turned! The free men of the world are marching together to victory.

"I have full confidence in your courage, devotion to duty and skill in battle. We will accept nothing less than full victory!

"Good luck. And let us all beseech the blessings of Almighty God upon this great and noble undertaking."

U.S. ARMY

69

The Clock Winds Down

And so now they go upon the waters of the English Channel, carried toward their—and the world's—destinies. They board the ships and leave the shore (below, that of Weymouth in Dorset). We know what Eisenhower said to his many men. That same day, Montgomery wrote a speech and instructed his commanders to read it to their troops. In 2012 a signed copy was discovered in England. He concluded with these words: "Good luck to each one of you. And good hunting on the mainland of Europe"—then quoted the Scottish nobleman and soldier James Graham:

> He either fears his fate
>   too much,
> Or his deserts are small,
> That dares not put it
>   to the touch,
> To win or lose it all.

To win or lose it all: That was what D-Day would be entirely about.

And now the Allies would put their fate—and ours—to the touch.

Overlord: The Drumbeat to D-Day

These generals were there with their men and women as this community—this *nation*—of warriors came together in England throughout the winter and spring of '44. They were there to inform, counsel, exhort, encourage and inspire (the essential things great leaders do). They had to change their plans more than once, since they didn't have enough landing craft to go on May 1. (Thirteen American shipyards were then told to produce a new one every day and a half, and they answered the call.) June 5 was now the day for Operation Neptune, the code name for the Normandy landings themselves, though for reasons we will learn, June 5 wouldn't be D-Day.

In the warrior nation were many Americans and British, of course, and Canadians, Frenchmen, Poles, Belgians, Greeks, Dutchmen, Norwegians and others, all with liberty on their minds and some with vengeance. They were having their last beers or glasses of wine before heading into battle, their last dates and farewell kisses. All were fretful, certainly, and many were fearful. They didn't know that the battle for Normandy would last more than two months, though they wouldn't have bet against it. They didn't know that there would be further and brutal fighting during what would be called the Battle of the Bulge, though they wouldn't have bet against it. They didn't know what was in store. They couldn't. And neither could Eisenhower, Roosevelt, Churchill, Stalin—or Hitler. But they all knew they were going.

And Hitler knew they were coming—somewhere.

ROBERT CAPA © INTERNATIONAL CENTER OF PHOTOGRAPHY/MAGNUM

The Longest Day

June 6, 1944, was, finally, the right day—and thus it would become known as D-Day, when Operation Overlord finally launched and took on a new and eternal designation.

By Douglas Brinkley

The Longest Day

On June 6, 1944, Franklin D. Roosevelt went to bed just after midnight. The D-Day invasion was under way, but the President was nevertheless determined to get a little shut-eye. His wife, Eleanor, was more anxious. She paced around the White House, waiting for General George C. Marshall to report on how the Allied forces fared on the five battlefield beaches of Normandy: Omaha and Utah (Americans), Gold and Sword (British), and Juno (Canadians). At three a.m., she woke up Franklin, who put on his favorite gray sweater and sipped some coffee before starting a round of telephone calls that lasted over five hours. When FDR finally held a press conference late that afternoon on the White House lawn, he talked about how distinctive D-Day was in world history. Crossing the turbulent waters of the English Channel from Dover to Pointe du Hoc with the largest armada in world history— the ships carried more than 100,000 American, British and Canadian soldiers—was truly an event for the ages. Later that evening Roosevelt addressed the world on the radio. He evoked the Fall of Rome before boasting that God had let the Allies prevail over the "unholy forces of our enemy" in Europe. Roosevelt was basking in the glow of one of history's seismic shifts.

The following day, June 7, newspapers were full of mind-boggling factoids and statistics about how D-Day had succeeded. One number that didn't appear was 36,525. Readers might guess that the number represents the tally of soldiers who landed at Omaha Beach or the number of ships and aircraft used in the cross-Channel operation or the number of German defenders or the number of casualties or any number of other things associated with Operation Overlord. But 36,525 is simply the number of days in a century, and of all the days in the 20th century, none were more consequential than June 6, 1944. Some might argue that certain inventions and discoveries during that great century of innovation should be deemed the most important—like Watson and Crick's reveal of the double-helix structure of DNA or all of Einstein's contributions—but other nominees flatten when one asks, "What if D-Day had failed?"

Usually, one day in a century rises above the others as an accepted turning point or historic milestone. It becomes the climactic day, or *the* day, of that century. For the 19th century, I'd choose July 3, 1863, when the youthful United States of America—split in two by a great Civil War—was finally set on the healing path that would allow it to remain a single nation. We can only imagine the history of the free world today if, at the end of the Civil War, there had been two countries: the United States and the Confederate States of America. And what date in the 18th century can beat July 4, 1776? In the 15th century, was there a more important date than October 12, 1492, when Christopher Columbus first sighted the New World? And the course of Western civilization was forever changed on October 14, 1066, when

The Longest Day

the Battle of Hastings brought William the Conqueror to England's throne. Almost a century and a half later, June 19, 1215, became the signature day of the 13th century when King John signed the Magna Carta, enumerating the rights of free men and establishing the rule of law.

The D-Day moniker wasn't invented for the Allied invasion. The same name had been attached to the date of every planned offensive of World War II. It was first coined during World War I, at the U.S. attack at the Battle of Saint-Mihiel, in France in 1918. The *D* was short for *day*. The expression literally meant "day-day" and signified the day of an attack. By the end of World War II, however, the phrase had become synonymous with a single date: June 6, 1944.

By the spring of 1944, as Daniel Levy and John Keegan have explained for us in eloquent detail, World War II had been raging for five tortuous years. If D-Day—the greatest amphibious operation ever undertaken—failed, there would be no going back to the drawing board for the Allies. Regrouping and attempting another massive invasion of German-occupied France even a few months later in 1944 wasn't an option. Historians must assume that if Operation Overlord had been a catastrophe, a major part of the Allied invasion force would have been destroyed, and it would have been no small task to rebuild it. The massive armada and matériel could not be replaced with the waving of a magic wand. There was not a second team on hand to step in and continue the job. In fact, the aspect of the Normandy invasion that sets it apart from all other operations in military history is that it had no backup plan. There was to be one throw of the dice against the German might. Before the attack, Supreme Allied Commander

Behind Enemy Lines

Below: In this photo, provided at the time by the U.S. Army Signal Corps, American paratroopers fix their static lines before a predawn jump over Normandy on June 6. Right: Same situation for hundreds more Americans, same place, same day. The decision to launch the airborne attack in darkness instead of waiting for first light was probably one of the few Allied missteps on D-Day, as the 82nd and 101st airborne divisions suffered heavy casualties in a situation quickly devolving into chaos. Approximately 13,100 U.S. paratroopers made night drops in the wee hours, and nearly 4,000 more were shuttled in by glider after daylight. This was all part of Operation Neptune, the assault phase of Overlord—but today we think of the whole as D-Day. There were a few ambitious goals for the paratroopers: to protect the amphibious attack forthcoming at Utah Beach; to secure exits off the beaches; to gain control of the Douve River so that Allied troops could cross; and ultimately to capture Cherbourg so the Allies would have a port of supply. In the event, the drops were too scattered and, for instance, the approaches to Utah—a preliminary assignment—wouldn't be secured for three days.

OPERATION OVERLORD, JUNE 6, 1944

Surprise was essential. For months the Allies successfully bluffed the Germans into believing they were going to attack farther north, and not along the 50-mile stretch of sand in Normandy, France. How to do it, though, proved to be a logistical nightmare, with the need to prepare the ships, build thousands of landing craft, gather the tanks, artillery and bulldozers, dispatch the special forces to scoop up French sand to determine if it could support heavy vehicles, quarantine the troops to make sure their loose lips wouldn't sink ships and pray for good weather. Prime Minister Winston Churchill appropriately called the D-Day invasion "undoubtedly the most complicated and difficult" attack ever undertaken. By late spring all was in order, and General Dwight D. Eisenhower commanded his Allied armada to capture Utah, Omaha, Gold, Juno and Sword beaches and free Europe from Nazi tyranny. Racing through the churning surf on June 6, the men met up against German machine guns and artillery, and the landings at Omaha and Juno beaches were especially bloody. Once they were ashore, the hard battle inland began.

U.S. First Army
General Bradley

U.S. VII Corps

U.S. 4th Infantry Div.

23,250 troops
300 casualties

U.S. V Corps

U.S. 29th & 1st Infantry Divs.

34,250 troops
2,400 casualties

CHERBOURG The Allies needed this deep-water port on the Cotentin Peninsula to bring in troops and supplies. As they battled their way there, Hitler ordered his commander to "leave to the enemy not a harbor but a field of ruin." Fighting raged for more than three weeks before the Americans captured it.

U.S. 82nd Airborne Div.
6,420 paratroopers with glider support
1,259 casualties

U.S. 101st Airborne Div.
6,928 paratroopers with glider support
1,240 casualties

U.S. AIRBORNE DIVISIONS More than 13,000 paratroopers from the 82nd and the 101st dropped into Normandy to prepare for the conquest of the Cotentin Peninsula by destroying bridges over the Douve River, securing areas near Utah Beach and capturing Sainte-Mère-Église, with its important road between Carentan and Cherbourg.

Cherbourg captured June 27

CHERBOURG

Fort du Roule

June 22

Cotentin Peninsula

VALOGNES

DDay_098-121_Longest6

June 12

June 18

SAINTE-MÈRE-ÉGLISE
June 6

UTAH

OMAHA

June 6

June 6

June 6

Battle of Carentan June 10–12

CARENTAN

LESSAY

PÉRIERS

June 12

July 1–24

Miles
km | 5 | 5 | 10

N
W — E
S

Casualty counts are estimates and represent the number of killed, wounded and missing in the initial D-Day assault.

SAINT-LÔ
Operation Cobra July 25–31

German Seventh Army

OPERATION COBRA Ashore for six weeks, the Allies grimly fought forward. General Omar Bradley decided he had to punch a hole in the German line. The bombing started July 25 as B-17s and B-24s blanketed the enemy. Major General Joseph "Lightning Joe" Collins's men then smashed through, and soon troops pushed across France. Bradley wrote Eisenhower, "Things on our front really look good."

MAP FOR LIFE BOOKS BY STEVE WALKOWIAK/SWMAPS.COM

Supreme Allied Commander General Eisenhower

21st Army Group General Montgomery

156,000 troops (73,000 U.S., 83,000 British and Canadian)

Naval personnel 195,700 Allied

English Channel

British Second Army Lieutenant General Dempsey

British I Corps

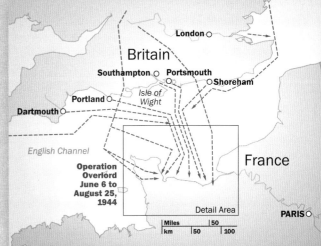

CROSSING THE CHANNEL Operation Neptune, the cross-Channel phase of the invasion, had to move 6,939 vessels and more than 100,000 troops across the open water. The convoys slipped from southern English ports, gathered off the Isle of Wight and then headed south to the Bay of the Seine, where they fanned out toward the beaches. Novelist and war correspondent Ernest Hemingway observed the landing and recalled how "the 36-foot coffin-shaped boats took solid green sheets of water that fell on the helmeted heads of the troops packed shoulder to shoulder in the stiff, awkward, uncomfortable, lonely companionship of men going to battle."

British XXX Corps

British 50th Infantry Div.

24,900 troops 400 casualties

Canadian 3rd Infantry Div.

21,400 troops 1,200 casualties

British 3rd Infantry Div.

28,845 troops 630 casualties

British 6th Airborne Div.

7,900 troops via parachute and glider 1,500 casualties

○ **LE HAVRE**

○ **DEAUVILLE**

LE HAVRE The Germans had turned this seaside community on the Seine River, just to the east of where the Allies landed, into an impregnable fortress. Armed blockhouses, bunkers and pillboxes lined the cliffs overlooking the Channel, and it was there that the German navy based a group of lethal torpedo boats.

GOLD   JUNO

SWORD

June 6

○ **BAYEUX**

June 12

Battle of Bréville June 7–13

Battle of Caen June 7–July 20

○ **CAEN**

July 1–24

Battle of Villers-Bocage June 13

F R A N C E

German Army Group B Field Marshal Rommel

ERWIN ROMMEL Like many other commanders, Rommel did not expect the invasion. On June 6, he was relaxing in Germany, celebrating his wife Lucie-Maria's birthday. That morning, when the Desert Fox learned what had happened, he exclaimed, "How stupid of me!" and rushed back to France. His forces slowed but could not stop the Allied onslaught, and the following month a strafing RAF Spitfire attacked his car and nearly killed him. When implicated soon after in a plot to kill Hitler, Rommel was allowed to bite into a cyanide pill in return for a promise that his family would be spared.

The Longest Day

Dwight D. Eisenhower confided to General Omar Bradley, "this operation is not being planned with any alternatives." Failure would also have meant that the chosen invasion site was forever compromised. There were already precious few suitable areas along the entire western European coast from Norway to southern France from which to choose an invasion site. After a long vetting process, the Allies finally settled on Normandy.

They did this even though the targeted areas had more negatives than positives overall. The curious topography of the Normandy beaches was anything but ideal for the landing of a naval craft that needed to drop bow ramps into the churning surf. The area was subject to the third-largest tidal fluctuations in the world, making amphibious operations treacherous. None of the five selected invasion beaches were well enough connected to the others to allow mutual assistance when the going got extra tough. The planned landing was the equivalent of making five separate attacks instead of advancing on a continuous battle line. Defeat at any one of those Normandy beaches could spell doom for the largest seaborne assault in world history. "The Allies were invading a continent where the enemy had immense capabilities for reinforcement and counterattack, not a small island cut off by sea power from sources of supply," U.S. naval historian Samuel Eliot Morison wrote. "Even a complete pulverizing of the Atlantic Wall at Omaha would have availed nothing if the German command had been given twenty-four hours' notice to move up reserves for counterattack. We had to accept the risk of heavy casualties on the beaches to prevent far heavier ones on the plateau and among the hedgerows."

There was no deep-water port to support this massive operation. It was one thing to put Allied troops ashore on

The Sun Rises

Below: Allied soldiers synchronize their watches prior to the invasion of Normandy on the sixth. Right: The American Navy cruiser USS *Augusta* lies off the invasion coast. It has steamed in almost within rifle range of the coast, and now covers landing craft speeding toward shore. Every ship has a story, and the *Augusta*'s—named for Augusta, Georgia—is a noble one. The cruiser had served throughout the world since her launch in 1930, and certainly would be part of Overlord. On the fifth, she stood out of Plymouth, England, with General Bradley and his staff aboard. On the sixth, her battery fired 51 rounds at German shore placements. Bradley and Co. left for new headquarters on the tenth, and the *Augusta* continued the fight. A bomb skirted her on the eleventh. On the twelfth, still anchored off Omaha Beach, she drove off an enemy plane, and on the thirteenth she shot down another. She continued to bomb the shore and provide antiaircraft defense deep into June. Then it was on to the Mediterranean. In 1945 she would usher President Truman across the Atlantic to the Potsdam Conference.

The Longest Day

a hostile beach, but keeping them there was quite another story. The supply requirements for food and ammunition were immense. To gain a foothold, the invading Allied army would require 400 tons of supplies each day to support just one infantry division, and a staggering 1,200 tons a day for each armored division. The initial assault was intended to have eight divisions land, but that was just the tip of the iceberg. The follow-up landings were to pour numerous other divisions ashore to form two armies.

And a landing at Normandy also meant that one of the great rivers of the world, the Seine, would be between the landing area and the objective—this being the industrial Rhine-Ruhr region leading into Nazi Germany. Rivers have proven to be great obstacles in military campaigns. A large, swollen river like the Seine would offer enemy defenders the opportunity to develop formidable lines.

Given all of these caveats, it's fair to wonder why Normandy was such an attractive location to President Roosevelt, Winston Churchill and the other Allied planners. The most convincing argument in the region's favor was its proximity to the supporting Allied airfields in southern England. A second advantage, ironically enough, was Normandy's perceived unsuitability as a landing site. Since it was fraught with clear disadvantages, it was deemed the least likely spot in the German mind and therefore afforded the Allies an opportunity for surprise. Surprise was absolutely essential for Operation Overlord's success because the Germans controlled the interior lines of communications and could quickly react to any threat by rushing reinforcements from far-flung locations in occupied France.

In 1944 the common appreciation for an amphibious assault had been graphically displayed in newsreel film as American audiences watched U.S. Marine assaults on

Storming the Beach

The original feisty 1944 caption for the photograph at left, below: "French Coast Dead Ahead. Helmeted Yankee soldiers crouch, tightly packed, behind the bulwarks of a Coast Guard landing barge in the historic sweep across the English Channel to the shores of Normandy. Minutes later, these GI Joes dashed through the surf and up the beach under the withering fire of Nazi defenders. These Coast Guard barges rode back and forth through D-Day bringing wave on wave of reinforcements to the beachhead." Below: A platoon of soldiers is transported to Omaha

Beach via a landing vehicle. On the following pages, American troops land on Omaha Beach, and we come now to the D-Day photography done for LIFE by the storied Robert Capa. Capa, who is seen amid the group of LIFE photographers pictured in our book's introduction (please see page 6), was in fact a Hungarian émigré named Endre Friedmann, who conspired in the 1930s to create the dashing persona of "Robert Capa," the world's preeminent war photographer, and then to expand upon it until Robert Capa was bigger than life. He was there at the Spanish Civil War, in China covering the fight against Japan, with U.S. troops in North Africa and Italy, and on a terrible Normandy beach on D-Day. He was with the first wave of troops when they landed in the face of furious resistance on Omaha. He shot four rolls of film, but a photo assistant in London ruined all but 11 images, which then were sent to LIFE's offices in New York City as quickly as technology would allow. They, and others from the Capa portfolio, are among the most famous photographs of war ever made. Capa's story continues in the caption on page 86.

The Longest Day

flyspeck islands in the central Pacific. Waves of landing craft broke upon the hostile beaches to initiate furious attacks against isolated Japanese defenders. The enemy rarely had air or naval support. The scenario became very familiar: Land the landing force; cut the island in half by driving to the other side; clear the first half and then clear the second half and, in the process, annihilate the defenders or drive them into the sea. It would all be over in days or weeks. Speed was of the essence.

But an amphibious landing at Normandy would be far different from landing on a tiny island like Wake or Iwo Jima in the central Pacific. This was the European continent, and the defenders were hardly isolated or lacking in reserves. In fact, the Third Reich had the ability to call upon up to 50 divisions in the vicinity of Normandy to react to an Allied attack.

An attack on the Normandy beaches can best be described as a showdown. Those beaches in northern France were the gates to the fortress, and if it was successful, then the entrance into the Continent would allow the military and industrial might of the Allies to pour onto the battlefield. That overwhelming might could then make victory a reasonable outcome. But if the attack failed, the consequences for democracy would be dire. The threat to Germany from the west would be over. Adolf Hitler would not have to fight on two fronts. Allied long-range air attacks against Germany would remain just that—long range—and Hitler's aircraft and rocket development could continue (as could the machinery of the Final Solution).

And what about the Soviet Union? Premier Joseph Stalin had made it clear that he had no intention of absorbing the losses and bloodletting of the war so that the Anglo-American alliance might come in at the end to reap the rewards. When Secretary of State Cordell Hull reminded his Soviet counterpart that the United States had not been unbloodied and indeed had suffered 200,000 casualties during the war, the Soviet diplomat abruptly cut him off, saying, "We lose that many each day before lunch." And didn't Russia bow out of World War I? What was to preclude another retreat and the conclusion of a separate understanding with Germany if it was advantageous to the Soviet Union? It had made deals with the devil before.

Exhausted from years of war, Europeans in 1944 longed for the day when they would be liberated from the totalitarian grip of Germany. There seemed to be no end in sight, and Great Britain had nearly depleted its reserves of manpower. It had fought alone in the Battle of Britain and had endured the naval Battle of the Atlantic. It had fought in Norway, North Africa and Sicily. It was now fighting in Italy and in the Pacific. On December 11, 1941, Adolf Hitler's sudden declaration of war against the United States brought Britain the hope of salvation. But while there was guarded jubilation among the beleaguered British, American involvement

Moments of Truth

Above: U.S. assault troops from the 1st Infantry Division's 16th Regiment wading through the waters of the English Channel to reach Omaha Beach during the D-Day invasion. Opposite, top: Soldiers of this same 1st Infantry Division struggle to get ashore at Omaha. Right: The same situation. This third photograph is, perhaps along with "Death of a Loyalist Soldier, Spain, 1936," Robert Capa's most famous (it is the picture on the cover of our book). There is very little about D-Day that is ironical, but irony attaches to Capa's 11 surviving images. As mentioned, his film underwent hazard when being processed in London. Most shots were ruined and the others were what might be called damaged. And yet, the grainy, shaky quality of the final printed images seems to conjure the quaking of the earth, or at least the beach. It seems as if a bomb had just landed at Capa's elbow: moments of truth, finding their truth inadvertently. Capa's pictures might have been the most evocative of the D-Day landing regardless of what befell them in the lab, but as rendered they immediately became a signature of what had occurred. (Many years later, film director Steven Spielberg used the Capa photographs as inspiration for the look and feel of the opening scene of *Saving Private Ryan*.) Capa, for all his dash and daring, freely admitted he shared the fears and fatigue of the men he accompanied in Normandy and elsewhere. During one campaign, he just kept repeating to himself, "I want to walk in the California sunshine and wear white shoes and white trousers." Indeed, all of this incredible evidence of war was produced by a man who hated armed conflict. "A war photographer's most fervent wish is for unemployment," he once said. But there is always one more war, and in 1954 he was in Japan when LIFE had need of a photographer in Indochina. Robert Capa, of course, volunteered, but he would step on a land mine there and be killed. He died with his camera in his hands.

The Longest Day

in the war initially changed little. In two years of indecisive Allied operations against the Wehrmacht, the Anglo-American team had been able to attack only the fringes of the German Reich. The main Allied success, as we have seen in these pages, had been taking control of North Africa.

Everyone, including Winston Churchill, knew that the road to the end of the war ran through Berlin. But no one was marching to Berlin without first invading the Continent. The incorrigible Churchill declared, "Unless we can go and land and fight Hitler and beat his forces on land, we shall never win this war."

On the other side, Hitler was equally astute concerning the inevitable Allied invasion attempt and the importance of defeating it: "Once defeated, the enemy will never again try to invade . . . They would need months to organize a fresh attempt."

Any Allied entry into Europe was going to be possible only by breaching the western wall of what had aptly been dubbed "Fortress Europe." In that respect, the Germans seemed to have all the military advantages. But the one advantage the Third Reich did not possess was superior intelligence capabilities. They were clueless as to where the invasion would come and could only speculate about potential landing sites. The Germans thought Calais the obvious landing point and made its beaches impregnable. Calais was situated less than 25 miles from the white cliffs of Dover across the English Channel, while the beaches of Normandy were 100 miles away.

The Germans had ignored Normandy, except for some basic defenses. Who would ever plan to land there? And if an attack were to come, how would it be supported without a port? General Dwight D. Eisenhower and his Supreme Headquarters Allied Expeditionary Force (SHAEF) team were encouraged to see only minor German defensive activity all along the windswept Norman coast. Nonetheless, the

The Beach Finally Behind Them

These are American assault troops of the 3rd Battalion, 28th Infantry Regiment, the first regiment to have traversed the sands of Omaha Beach and gained the comparative safety of the chalk cliffs, which are at their back. Medics who landed with the troops are treating the minor injuries of those who will continue up and then onward. This picture was made on June 8, as Operation Overlord continued in the wake of D-Day. From the LIFE account of the Normandy invasion in June 1944: "By the afternoon of D-Day plus one, the battle of this beachhead was already the most desperate of the invasion. The Germans had set up machine-gun positions atop the bluffs; and these, with ingeniously concealed batteries, had raked landing parties. Casualties of some of the assault forces had been high." On the following pages, another photograph by Robert Capa, of American dead on the beachheads of Normandy.

The Longest Day

only chance for the operation's success was to keep everything top secret. Eisenhower had succeeded in his role as Allied commander by remaining tight-lipped. If he hadn't carefully cultivated a culture of trust between Americans and Britons, then Operation Overlord would have been doomed before it even began.

But "leak proofing" is easier said than done, especially when it comes to the "when" and "where" of a massive invasion like D-Day. The enemy is usually tipped off by invasion preparations—the most obvious being the use of aerial bombing and naval gunfire to soften up the site. Eisenhower decided that secrecy trumped softening, so the days and weeks preceding the landings were marked by silence instead of preinvasion bombardment.

The Great Secret would also be safeguarded by the unleashing of a monumental Allied deception plan, designed to convince the Germans that the invasion would occur at a location other than Normandy. Part of that deception included the efforts of 28 middle-aged British officers, who settled in to a castle in the far reaches of Scotland with radios and operators. They planted fear in the German mind of the existence of a massive 250,000-man force:

Other Beaches, Other Battles, Other Allies

Below: British commando troops landing on Sword Beach on June 6. Opposite, top: Troops from the 48th Royal Marines at Saint-Aubin-sur-Mer on Juno Beach on D-Day. Bottom: Soldiers of the 9th Canadian Infantry Brigade swarm ashore at Bernières-sur-Mer. Sword, Juno and Gold beaches, stretching west for 22 miles from the mouth of the Orne River, were largely the assignment of the British and Canadian armies, with troops contributed from other sympathetic nations and freedom fighters from occupied nations. They started landing at approximately 7:30 on the sixth, about an hour later than the Americans. Sword Beach was supposedly the most heavily defended of the three, but after ferocious initial fighting the Allies made quick progress. (Later, the people of Colleville-sur-Orne renamed their town Colleville-Montgomery in appreciation of the British general.) It turned out that Juno, the middle beach, was the toughest to take. General H.D.G. Crerar's Canadian 3rd Division, which was part of the British I Corps, as was the division engaged on Sword, was pummeled by artillery fire. That assault lasted a half hour, but then the Canadians, too, moved forward. On Gold Beach at Ver-sur-Mer, the British 50th Infantry needed only 15 minutes to clear the beach. If the Americans led the D-Day assault, their comrades in arms shared the day equally with them.

D-Day Is Understood

Both of these photographs were made on June 6. At left is an aerial view of American troops and tanks moving ashore in Normandy as landing craft continue to unload. At right, below: General Alfred Jodl, Germany's chief of operations staff of the Armed Forces High Command (and, incidentally, the man who would later sign his country's unconditional surrender), points out Allied landing areas to his Führer, Hitler, while other members of the High Command, including Hermann Göring (light uniform) and Joachim von Ribbentrop (top left) look on. It is improbable that any of the men in this conclave registered surprise or dismay—it was not the Nazi way—but surely all of them *were* surprised and dismayed and were now scrambling for a plan. Elsewhere, the U.S.S.R.'s Stalin was certainly pleased: In one morning, a second front had been established, and the Third Reich had to look west as well as east. Churchill and Roosevelt were pleased that this plan without a backup was going forward, largely as planned, despite the paratroop problems. Eisenhower was pleased that Operation Overlord, as envisaged, seemed sound in execution.

General Jodl is not as famous as some of his Nazi confreres, but he met a fate shared by several of them. Charged at the postwar Nuremberg trials with conspiracy, crimes against peace, war crimes (he had ordered prisoner executions) and crimes against humanity, he was convicted of all counts and hanged on October 16, 1946. Göring and von Ribbentrop, too, would be handed death sentences in Nuremberg. There will be more about that later in our book.

the British Fourth Army, which was capable of invading Norway. Their phony network traffic—purposely communicated in a low-level cipher that they knew the listening Germans could easily break—included requests for cold-weather gear and equipment.

If the D-Day invasion was to have a chance to succeed, the Germans would have to be continually misled. Churchill had told FDR that in wartime "Truth is so precious that she must often be attended by a bodyguard of lies."

That bodyguard of lies led to the creation of many bizarre operations, not the least of which was the creation of a second, semifictitious Army group stationed in and around Dover. It was commanded by General George S. Patton, whom the German military leadership considered the best Allied combat leader. Wherever Patton was stationed, the Germans believed, the big invasion would surely follow. That meant they thought the cross-Channel attack would take place from Dover to Calais. At Dover, fake camps were constructed and tents erected to create the illusion that American soldiers were occupying them. Loudspeakers transmitted the recorded sounds of vehicles, tanks and camp activities that escaped through the trees and were heard in the surrounding towns. Guards were posted at the entrances and vehicles regularly moved in and out, but few people were actually actively engaged inside those gates.

Contributing to the deception were a whole host of agents and double agents all tasked to obscure and confuse. One such agent was the master of deception Juan Pujol Garcia, a Spaniard who assumed the code name Garbo. Posing as a German agent, he had created his own fictitious spy network of 20 operatives who supposedly fed him information about the Allies. Much of it was tantalizing and laced with elements of truth, but he passed it on to the Germans in such

The Longest Day

a fashion as to cause minimal damage to the Allied cause. Yet his accuracy was astounding to the Germans, and as a result he built impressive bona fides with the Abwehr (the German military intelligence). One of the many results of the deception plan was convincing Hitler that the Allies had 89 divisions when, in fact, they had only 47.

But despite all of the cloak-and-dagger work, Eisenhower still had to get the invading force ashore. That was no easy task at Normandy. Unlike other landing areas, Normandy has an enormous tidal wash that, twice a day, floods the beaches and then recedes. The 20-foot difference in elevation between low tide and high means that at high tide the water is 300 yards farther inland than at low. At high tide, the water covered the beach and the German obstacles and lapped at the wall.

Eisenhower planned to land at dead low tide, on five isolated beaches across a 60-mile front. Four of the beaches—Omaha, Gold, Juno and Sword—were enclaves along the Norman coast. The fifth was figuratively out on the end of a limb, alone on the Cotentin Peninsula, 15 miles south of Cherbourg. It was named Utah Beach and, while a successful landing there would position the attackers to make a run to seize the deep-water port of Cherbourg, Allies who landed there would be the most vulnerable. Their only protection from an annihilating German counterattack would be if the two American airborne divisions, the 82nd and 101st, could drop and seize the narrow causeways that led to the beach across flooded fields.

Eisenhower was also faced with having to move the entire armada across the widest part of the English Channel, thereby increasing its possible discovery. He had to isolate the battlefield where he intended to land. He was confident that his force could deal with any military forces

Inch by Inch

Below are German troops defending their position in Normandy during the Allied D-Day invasion, and at right are American troops with German prisoners of war on Omaha Beach on June 6. From LIFE's contemporaneous account, which was written by Charles Christian Wertenbaker: "From the bluff you could see beyond the beach almost 12 miles to sea, and all this expanse of water was filled with boats . . . About five miles out lay the cruisers and battleships, pumping salvos of high explosive into the enemy batteries inland. Yet in spite of their noise, and sharper sounds of enemy shells and our demolition charges on the beach, in spite of the wreckage and movement of men and machines across the beach, you could not fail to see the beauty of the scene to seaward. The Channel was as blue as the Mediterranean, and as still. In the blue, cloudless sky above it floated hundreds of silver barrage balloons, twinkling in the sunlight."

already within the confines of the battlefield, but it was imperative to keep reserves and reinforcements from entering into the fray, especially during the early hours of invasion, when the attack was still feeble. To do that he called upon the air forces to disrupt and destroy the German ability to move. The British Royal Air Force and the United States Army Air Corps would bomb and attack bridges, railcars, rolling stock, train yards and tracks—essentially any target that could be used to transport German reserves to the battlefield. Eisenhower labeled this simply the Transportation Plan.

But here, he ran into a thorny problem—not from the enemy, but from his own British and American air officers. They contended that the execution of the air offensive should be left to them and that bombing transportation targets would greatly impair their ongoing Oil Plan. They believed that if oil supplies, refineries and storage facilities could be annihilated, then the German war machine would grind to a halt. Unlike Eisenhower, they didn't place transportation infrastructure high on the list of priority targets.

But Ike knew that the Transportation Plan would result in only a temporary halt of the Oil Plan. As Supreme Commander, he scoffed at the idea that he was not in charge of making determinations about the air forces. The air chiefs, however, did not share this belief and interpreted Eisenhower's duties and responsibilities as limited to command on the ground and at sea. Even Churchill sided with

the air chiefs concerning the Oil Plan, but as the crisis mounted, it was Eisenhower who brought the argument to an abrupt halt. As Supreme Commander, he was ultimately responsible for the success or failure of the operation. Unless he was given control of the bombers to use as he saw fit to accomplish his mission, take care of his men and win at Normandy, he would "simply have to go home."

He won the argument. He unleashed the Transportation Plan on the Wehrmacht and, in the run-up to D-Day, destroyed 900 locomotives, more than 16,000 railcars and countless miles of track. The Oil Plan was later resumed with enormous success.

Solving the problem of the lack of a deep-water port was more daunting. Such existing ports were at Cherbourg, Dieppe and Calais and were heavily defended. A failed August 1942 raid on the small French port of Dieppe had proven just how well defended. The attack was a calamity for the Allies that resulted in more than 4,000 Canadian casualties. Nazi newspapers had cheered about Hitler's forces decisively beating a huge invasion attempt.

The final answer to the port problem came in the form of an engineering marvel code-named Mulberry. Never before had an army tried to take its harbors with it to an invasion beach. A large consortium of British engineering companies tackled the problem of building two floating artificial harbors, each of which would have the unloading capacity of the Port of Dover. That port had taken seven years to build,

Upward, Then Onward

Opposite: U.S. B-26 Marauders (which, although you can't see them, sport special D-Day markings) fly over the beaches of Cherbourg, laying smoke screen in advance of the Allied landings. Right: On July 11, an American GI fires a howitzer at retreating German forces. Gaining the high ground in Normandy was difficult, as had been anticipated. From Wertenbaker's on-the-scene account for LIFE: "A narrow, dusty road twisted up from the beach to the bluff. Up it wound a column of men and vehicles. They moved slowly past signs saying, 'Achtung, Minen,' keeping to the road, to the top. There, overlooking the beautiful seascape with its twinkling balloons, was a cluster of large mass graves, and near them men were digging fresh ones. Beside the road a soldier lay full-length on his face, his arms outstretched."

CORBIS

The Longest Day

but these floating ports had to be ready in 150 days. If the invasion proved successful, various parts of the Mulberry harbors would be towed across the English Channel to Normandy, where they would be assembled to make the two giant seaports.

The window of opportunity to launch this enormous

attack was indeed a narrow one. There were four prerequisites. First was the tide. Eisenhower wanted to land on a late spring or early summer morning so he could use the night to conceal his seaborne approach to the Norman coast (and obscure his unloading operations). An early dawn landing offered some promise of surprise, and it would give him a full

day of fighting to secure a foothold in France. The second consideration was the moon. The navy needed some light to maneuver the massive armada at sea, and the paratroopers would need at least some moonlight to allow them to find each other on the ground in the fields of France. The bombardiers also needed light to see and identify their targets.

The third and fourth prerequisites had to do with training. The 1944 landing would have to come early enough in the summer to allow a minimum of three months of good campaigning weather before the onset of winter, but it had to be late enough in the year to allow for the completion of training and, as we have learned, the construction

Gaining Ground, Establishing Command

Left: On June 9, American troops still on Utah Beach take a breather after reaching the comparative safety offered by a concrete wall. Above: U.S. troops and equipment are scattered about a command post on Red Beach, one of 10 code-named sectors of Omaha, on June 8. All these years later, the reporting in the LIFE account of the day still rings accurate: "Although the extent of the U.S. casualties in the Normandy landings has not yet been announced, they were generally lighter than expected. The wounded have received magnificent care. The evacuation chain set up by Major General Paul R. Hawley, head ETO surgeon, appeared to be working smoothly. Invasion reporters who never got to France at all found a minor epic in the return of the wounded to English ports on the day after the first assault. Some of them walked off the ships with their uniforms torn and their bandages hastily applied, but safely and swiftly carried out of the battle zone. Others came on stretchers carried by Negro litter bearers, their personal belongings piled beside them. Some carried their boots, with French sand still clinging to the soles, on their litters. Many spoke of the fine work done by medical men on the beaches. Said one man, 'They're right in there, giving morphine and bandaging wounds while the bullets whiz past their ears.'"

At left are British infantrymen storming German positions during the invasion, and below is a prisoner being taken. Things are going well. From the second LIFE issue printed after D-Day: "Last week was a week to remember. All the way across a hemisphere—along the green hedgerows of Normandy, in the mountains of old Italy, through the jungles of Burma, and on the islands of the Pacific—the fires of war blazed up with new and steady fury. Everywhere on the battlefronts of the world-wide war, America's armed might was making itself felt.

"In France the British and Americans deepened their beachhead against the 16 German divisions deployed against them. Cherbourg had still not been captured but the Americans had cut the peninsula and were close to taking the big port. Marshal Stalin said of the Second Front he so long desired, 'The large-scale forcing of the English Channel and the mass landing of troops of the allies in northern France have fully succeeded. One must admit that the history of wars does not know any such undertaking so broad in conception and so grandiose in its scale and so masterly in execution.'"

of enough landing vessels, particularly the LSTs (Landing Ship, Tank). LSTs—what one officer described as "a large, empty, self-propelled box"—were the linchpins of D-Day. There were well over 40 different types of these landing craft used in the invasion.

Those four major restrictions left only a few options in all of 1944 for possible invasion days. The first opportunity would be on May 1, followed by a few days during the first and third weeks in June. The Allies had set May 1 as D-Day, but immediately had to cancel when it became evident that the invasion was short 271 LSTs. Hopefully one month's delay would allow for the production of those additional ships. Churchill reportedly growled that the destinies of the "two greatest empires seemed to be tied up in some god-damn thing called LSTs." But Eisenhower set D-Day back to June 5 to have more of the vessels at his disposal.

The month of May brought gorgeous weather to Normandy. General Eisenhower was encouraged and moved his headquarters from London to Southwick House, near Portsmouth. Upon arrival, he sent a coded message to all his chief commanders: "Exercise Hornpipe plus six." That meant that June 5 was still confirmed as D-Day. He sent a second message to Washington: "Halcion plus 4," meaning precisely the same thing.

But as fate would have it, almost as soon as Eisenhower sent those encouraging missives, signals arrived from American planes flying weather missions over Newfoundland. They

showed that conditions were drastically changing off the East Coast of the United States. A great swirling front was developing, and this disruptive weather system was labeled "L5."

By June 3, though the weather was beautiful over the English Channel, L5 was becoming a major problem. The chief of SHAEF's meteorological team, Group Captain James M. Stagg of the British Royal Air Force, followed its trajectory and then alerted Eisenhower that the weather prospects were not good. In fact, there was a possibility of Force 5 winds on June 4 and 5. Stagg reported that the whole North Atlantic was filled with a succession of depressions of a severe nature theretofore unrecorded in more than 40 years of modern meteorological research. He recommended postponing the operation.

A disappointed Eisenhower grilled Stagg and made a reluctant, provisional decision to postpone D-Day. His final decision would be made after the 4:15 meeting on the morning of June 4. The 6,000 ships of the invasion force were all in position, with the soldiers having been embarked for several days. Some vessels had even started the long crossing. The cross-Channel attack was like a drawn bowstring, straining for release, and L5 was in the way.

By 4:15, nothing had changed. At the meeting, Eisenhower polled his staff. Some bullheaded advisers wanted to go full throttle to Normandy, bad weather be damned. Others did not. The Allied Navy, under the command of Admiral Bertram Ramsay, said it would be unaffected by high winds and chop. But the planes would have a major problem, especially the troop carriers in charge of delivering the paratroopers. Without the paratroopers protecting the approaches to Utah Beach, that landing would have to be called off. Eisenhower postponed D-Day until June 6. The great armada, already at sea, was called back. The paratroopers were stood down for 24 hours, and Eisenhower and his staff would again meet at 21:30.

At 21:30, Stagg's predicted gale-force winds were driving the pouring rain horizontally into the windowpanes of Southwick House, the estate that served as the site of SHAEF's Advance Command Post. As Stagg entered the tension-filled room, he surprisingly modified his gloomy predictions and reported that despite the present stormy weather, the cloud conditions would improve and the winds would lessen after midnight. The weather would be tolerable, but no better than that.

Again Eisenhower polled his lieutenants, who were still divided. He finally declared, "I'm quite positive the order must be given . . . I don't like it, but there it is." Operation Overlord slipped back into gear, and the great armada rolled out into the English Channel. On June 5, Eisenhower left himself one last opportunity to recall the invasion at an early morning meeting scheduled for six hours later. At that 4:15 gathering, nothing had changed. Eisenhower gave the final order in three brisk words: "Okay, let's go."

Beyond the Beaches

D-Day—the day itself—was largely about the amphibious assault with air cover. But all Allied commanders knew that there would be many days of fight beyond D-Day. Berlin was not in Normandy, after all, and therefore the push had to continue, and resistance at every turn in the rutted road—or every field or every hedgerow—was to be expected. Here, American soldiers dig foxholes on June 10, shortly after gaining higher ground in Normandy. From LIFE: "When U.S. troops broke into the outworks of Cherbourg last week, they began the last operation in the first stage of the Battle for France. When Cherbourg fell the Allied toehold on the Continent would become a full-fledged battlefront instead of a narrow beachhead. With the Allies in possession of Cherbourg's fine roadstead, sheltered from the sea by its granite breakwaters, the tenuous beach supply line would become a firm, pulsating artery. Then the Allies could bring the full weight of their military superiority to bear against the weakening German Reich." So Cherbourg was the target, but so were the hearts and souls of the French: "The people of Manche and Calvados who had fled their homes during the fighting, now were coming back. They were friendly but they had a certain provincial reserve. Many greeted the troops with mixed emotions. The Allies, after all, had brought the war with them."

BETTMANN/CORBIS

Below are troops of the 2nd Infantry Division, filing up the bluff from the Easy Red sector of Omaha Beach after the D-Day invasion has succeeded. Opposite: General Omar Bradley (seated, left) and Admiral Alan Kirk going ashore in Normandy. Bradley was a hero: From the beginning of D-Day through the fall of Berlin he commanded all U.S. ground forces invading from the west—1.3

ULLSTEIN BILD/GRANGER

million men, the largest body of American servicemen ever to serve under one field commander. Five people have ascended to the rank of five-star general in the U.S. Armed Forces. Bradley was the last.

In the end, the weather didn't terribly disrupt the D-Day landings, and the blustery conditions lulled the Nazi defenders into thinking that an Allied attack was impossible. The invasion began on the wings of the airborne assault and its 21,100 paratroopers. On the eastern edge of the invasion area, the British 6th Airborne Division came in to seize and control key bridges to keep any German counterattack from striking the flank at Sword Beach and rolling up the invasion. On the west side of the battlefield, the American airborne dropped in to seize the towns of Carentan and Sainte-Mère-Église in order to control the road networks leading to Utah Beach.

The American sky train that flew to Normandy comprised 850 troop carriers. They flew in a formation nine planes wide and 300 miles long. It took great skill to avoid midair collisions, and radio silence was strictly maintained. A tiny blue dot on the tail of each aircraft was all that a pilot could see of the plane to his front. British air marshal Trafford Leigh-Mallory had confided to Eisenhower that he thought up to 70 percent of the paratroopers could be killed, wounded or captured.

Eisenhower had joined these paratroopers at their airfields and remained until the last C-47s had disappeared into the night before retiring to his small trailer near Southwick House. He penned a note to be released if the invasion failed: "Our landings . . . have failed. And I have withdrawn the troops. My decision to attack at this time and place was based on the best information available. The

Survivors, and Others

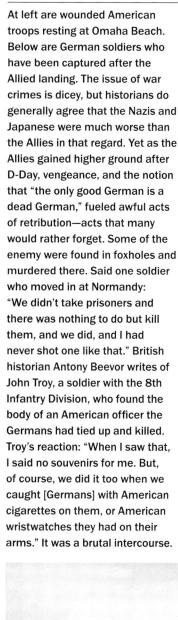

At left are wounded American troops resting at Omaha Beach. Below are German soldiers who have been captured after the Allied landing. The issue of war crimes is dicey, but historians do generally agree that the Nazis and Japanese were much worse than the Allies in that regard. Yet as the Allies gained higher ground after D-Day, vengeance, and the notion that "the only good German is a dead German," fueled awful acts of retribution—acts that many would rather forget. Some of the enemy were found in foxholes and murdered there. Said one soldier who moved in at Normandy: "We didn't take prisoners and there was nothing to do but kill them, and we did, and I had never shot one like that." British historian Antony Beevor writes of John Troy, a soldier with the 8th Infantry Division, who found the body of an American officer the Germans had tied up and killed. Troy's reaction: "When I saw that, I said no souvenirs for me. But, of course, we did it too when we caught [Germans] with American cigarettes on them, or American wristwatches they had on their arms." It was a brutal intercourse.

troops, the air and the Navy did all that bravery and devotion to duty could do. If any blame attaches to the attempt it is mine alone."

The great sky train flew to the west of the Cotentin Peninsula and then turned to the east to cut across the narrow neck of land. Its approach was greeted by a heavy German antiaircraft barrage. Many men described the colorful display of tracers streaming up through the night as if they were Roman candles. When the flak struck the aircraft, it sounded like nails being thrown against the sides. The intense fire caused many aircraft to swerve to avoid midair collisions and others to increase their speeds to escape the streams of green and yellow fingers reaching into the sky.

The air over France was filled with parachuting soldiers. It was also filled with falling debris—burning aircraft, detached rifles, helmets and packs ripped from the troopers by the impact of their parachutes opening. The drop was badly scattered, and paratroopers landed in trees, hedgerows, farm fields and on barns. Very few landed in their designated zones, but they were able to adapt thanks to their training and discipline. Some troopers joined other units and fought until they could find their own squads and platoons. Others attacked the Germans wherever they could find them. They all struggled to seize the causeways and gain control of the roads.

At two a.m. on June 6, the ships of the great armada halted 12 miles off the Normandy coast and began disembarking their soldiers into landing craft. The gigantic fleet had crossed the English Channel undetected and, by three

ROBERT CAPA © INTERNATIONAL CENTER OF PHOTOGRAPHY/MAGNUM

GRANGER

o'clock, the small landing craft were already circling, awaiting their run to the beach. Then and only then came the prebombardment of the invasion area. There was one hour of battleship and heavy-ship naval gunfire, followed by one hour of a 2,000-plane bombing offensive.

The landing craft finally began their run-in to the five invasion beaches. Because of the diagonal direction of the incoming tide, the American beaches were assaulted at 6:30, one hour before the British beaches to the east. The American 4th Infantry Division landed at Utah Beach with its armor in the lead to easily sweep aside the small German defending force. The infantry came in next and moved off the beach. By noon they had linked up with the elements of the 101st Airborne that had earlier sealed off the approaches to the beach. The landings at Utah succeeded beyond the wildest expectations of the Allied planners; the combined air and sea assault had worked perfectly despite the scattered paratroop drop. Leigh-Mallory's prediction that 70 percent of the paratroopers could be lost was, thankfully, off the mark. There were many fewer casualties, and the landing had generally surprised the German sentries.

Thirty miles to the east of Utah Beach, the American assault regiments of the 1st and 29th Infantry Divisions approached Omaha Beach, which was dominated by a looming 100-foot cliff. It was at this location that Field Marshal Erwin Rommel had recognized this beach as a possible invasion site and ordered it fortified. For the next few months, the Germans had constructed concrete-and-steel defensive positions. There were 15 of these massively strong positions, called *Widerstandsnests*, covering the entire length of the six-mile beach, each bearing a number from 59 to 74.

Unlike at Utah Beach, the first wave to land at Omaha did so without armor. Only five of the 32 tanks assigned to the landing site made it to the beach, and those were immediately destroyed. The German fire along the beach was tremendous, especially from the Widerstandsnests, and the American line was broken. The Americans had run into a wall of steel, and camouflaged guns fired an enfilading crisscross pattern across the entire length of the beach. Twenty minutes later, there were few men who were not dead or wounded. And then, on their heels, came the second and third waves, each destined to meet the same fate.

The Americans were pinned down. Some hid behind beach obstacles. All along the beach, small groups attempted to crawl forward, knowing that salvation would be found off the beach. American officers ran up and down, yelling at the men to move out and telling them that the only way to survive was to get up to high ground. In twos and fours they crawled and clawed their way through barbed wire and mines to the sloping ground. With the help of direct fire from daring American destroyers, the Americans slowly pushed the Germans out of their positions. By 11 o'clock,

CORBIS

MARIE HANSEN

The Good News Is Delivered

On the opposite page, military staff at LaGuardia Field in New York City gather around a radio and listen intently as President Franklin D. Roosevelt prays for the Allied invaders of Normandy on D-Day. Top: Winston Churchill struts to Parliament to announce the D-Day landings and their apparent success. Above: Roosevelt at the White House after the invasion, his mood reflected in his mien. There could be no spinning after Operation Overlord was launched: It had succeeded or it hadn't—and it meant much either way. It had succeeded.

The Longest Day

the fire on the beach was diminished. A little after noon, the beach was mostly quiet.

But the effort to win at Omaha came at a tremendous cost. There were more than 2,000 casualties. The beach was strewn with wrecked vehicles and burning ships and boats. Some infantry units had lost most of their officers and many of their soldiers. The fight on that beach earned the name Bloody Omaha.

In the center of the invasion area, just four miles west of Omaha Beach, was a strange and dangerous place called Pointe du Hoc. It was a point of land that stuck out into the English Channel and rose 100 feet above the water between Omaha and Utah beaches. The Germans had fortified this promontory with large, 150mm guns that were able to fire on both beaches and therefore threaten the entire invasion. Eisenhower knew that this fortification had to be taken and ordered the Rangers of the 2nd and 5th Battalions to eliminate the threat. Unlike at the beaches, Pointe du Hoc had no shoreline. The Rangers would have to scale the steep cliffs to attack the guns.

"When we went into battle after all this training there was no shaking of the knees or weeping or praying," U.S. lieutenant James Eikner of Mississippi recalled. "We knew what we were getting into. We knew every one of us had volunteered for extra hazardous duty. We went into battle

Below, left: On June 12, 1944, less than a week after D-Day, Prime Minister Winston Churchill crosses the English Channel on the destroyer HMS *Kelvin* to visit the invasion beaches, and the men still there, in Normandy. Such an occurrence would

GRANGER

have been, only hours before, unthinkable to the leaders of the Third Reich (and probably to those of the Allied forces). Below is a column of German troops captured on D-Day, being marched in Bernières-sur-Mer, Normandy—another eventuality that would have been seen as a nightmare by the Nazis. D-Day truly did turn the world around. Everyone knew it was coming, but nobody knew what it might mean. Suddenly, in a heartbeat, what it might mean was made crystal clear.

confident . . . We were intent on getting the job done. We were actually looking forward to accomplishing our mission." No matter how many oral histories are collected about D-Day, it's still impossible to understand what each man felt as he crossed the English Channel. There was not a singular kind of war experience for the survivors of that day.

Arriving in eight landing craft, the Rangers fired hooks and grapnels with attached ropes from mortar tubes on the boats. When they snagged on the barbed wire or the ground on top of the cliff, the Rangers began to climb, hand over hand. Once at the top, they attacked the surprised Germans, swept them aside and rushed to the fortifications to silence the guns. But the concrete casements had no guns. In their place were protruding telephone poles disguised to look like guns in order to deceive aerial photography.

The Rangers secured the position and moved inland to block the coastal road that ran behind all the invasion beaches. But two Rangers reconnoitered a dirt path that ran between the hedgerows separating the farm fields. A short distance down the road, they found real guns, well hidden under camouflage netting and aimed at Utah Beach. The Germans had no idea that there were any Americans within miles of their position, and while the gun crews were at the far end of the field listening to a

Prisoners

The assault had been effective, which was the crucial point. In these rare color photographs, German prisoners of war have been put behind barbed wire on Omaha Beach (below, with an LST and barrage balloons visible in the background), and German prisoners of war are on board a landing craft transport (right), prepared for delivery to a Liberty Ship in the English Channel, which will ferry them part of the way to prison—for the short term. The war in the Pacific had some miles left to be run. The war in Europe was tilting decisively toward the Allies, but, of course, a war is not over until the surrender is signed. And Hitler, reading no tea leaves, was hardly ready to surrender.

GALERIE BILDERWELT/GETTY (2)

The Tolling

At left is a landing craft loaded with American wounded at a beach in Normandy, wounded who will be quickly transferred to a hospital ship offshore. These men will receive treatment at field hospitals, then will be evacuated to make room for other casualties expected. Below are American Army glider pilots, on June 8, who were among the very first combatants during the D-Day invasion, relaxing and smoking cigarettes while aboard landing craft that are returning them to England after they have accomplished their mission objectives. The losses on both sides were never negligible. The leaders who sent the Allied troops into battle, including Roosevelt and Churchill, knew this would be so. The thinking was: whatever was needed.

German officer issuing orders, the Rangers squeezed through the hedges and disabled the guns with thermite grenades before creeping out. The guns were eliminated. Though the Germans furiously counterattacked the Rangers for the next two days, the Rangers held on. Those five German guns, capable of wreaking havoc on the invasion force, remained silent on D-Day.

Farther to the east, the Canadian 3rd Division approached Juno Beach. But because of buffeting currents and difficult navigation, their landing craft arrived after the rising tide had covered many of the beach obstacles. The boats began to strike these obstacles, which were called tetrahedrons, hedgehogs and Belgian gates. Great pilings had been anchored in the sand with mines attached to the tips. As the boats snagged on them or had their bottoms ripped out or exploded, the vessels sank, taking their embarked soldiers with them. Whole boat teams were lost in the surf of Juno Beach.

From the land, German defenders fired on the boats that managed to avoid the mines, until some of the Canadian soldiers finally landed and were able to push through the shallow German defenses. But half of their boats had been damaged, and more than a third forever lost. By late morning, the Canadian division had gained control of the beach, but at a cost of more than 1,000 men.

The British landings at Sword and Gold beaches were huge successes. The British 3rd and 50th Divisions made

great progress and moved aggressively inland from their beaches. By two o'clock, elements of the British amphibious forces from Sword had linked up with the 6th Airborne, which was protecting the east flank of the invasion area. The forces at Gold Beach achieved most of their objectives and were the only unit to link up with an adjacent beach when they joined forces with the Canadians on Juno. "D-Day was a success, and the Allies had breached Hitler's seawall," President Ronald Reagan noted on the 38th anniversary of the Normandy invasion. "They swept into Europe, liberating towns and cities and countrysides until the Axis powers were finally crushed. We remember D-Day because the French, British, Canadians and Americans fought shoulder to shoulder for democracy and freedom—and won."

As D-Day ended, the Allies were far short of the grand objectives that had been optimistically set for the day. The

Fallen Soldiers

The dead on the opposite page are Americans, and below are German prisoners burying men killed during and after D-Day. All of this death had been anticipated by Roosevelt, Churchill and Eisenhower. In fact, the death toll wasn't as egregious as it might have been—egregious though it certainly was. Once it had been decided that Operation Overlord would be put in force, great loss of life was inevitable (even if the outcome of the assault was not). It is meager to say when talking about something so immense as D-Day: It all went pretty well. The Allies carried the day, pushed upward and onward and let Berlin know that any kind of final showdown would be of its choosing. Paris was in the Allied sights, and so was Germany. D-Day was hardly behind the troops—it never would or could be—but D-Day had been a success as absolute as Eisenhower or anyone might have hoped. How does one get to the top of those cliffs, with gunfire raining down? How was that achieved? The Allies surmounted the cliffs, ran across the fields of the high ground and set their sights on Germany and ultimate victory. Yes, but when they were running across those fields, they perhaps thought the end would come easy. The end would not come easy.

The Longest Day

old aphorism that "no plan survives first contact with the enemy" held true. But the Allies were dug in all across the front, and the German army had not been able to hurl them back into the sea. These young soldiers didn't know that they still faced seven weeks of hard fighting before the Normandy campaign would be won. But in those next seven weeks, through newsreels and photography, the world followed them through the shattered French villages, first to capture Cherbourg and finally to break out of Normandy at Saint-Lô. You see that imagery on these pages. Cameras captured Allied forces as they were greeted every step of the way by the suddenly free French people.

A young French girl who had sought to help the wounded on Sword Beach that D-Day morning saw the war's end in sight. To her, D-Day was the moment when liberty was reclaimed for the world. She said, "When I saw the invasion fleet, it was something that you just can't imagine. It was boats, boats, boats and boats at the end, boats at the back, and the planes coming over. If I had been a German, I would have looked at this, put my arms down, and said, 'That's it. Finished!'"

DOUGLAS BRINKLEY IS A PROFESSOR OF HISTORY AT RICE UNIVERSITY AND AUTHOR OF *THE BOYS OF POINTE DU HOC: RONALD REAGAN, D-DAY, AND THE U.S. ARMY 2ND RANGER BATTALION* AND *VOICES OF VALOR: D-DAY, JUNE 6, 1944* (WITH RONALD J. DREZ).

In Memoriam

At left, on June 14, 1944, at Colleville-sur-Mer in Normandy, formerly code-named and forever remembered by Americans as Omaha Beach, local French residents join in a Mass in memory of the soldiers killed, barely a week before, during the D-Day landings. Opposite: The following month, on the eve of the Fourth of July, a U.S. Army bugler plays "Taps" during a religious service to inaugurate a special cemetery for American soldiers who died during the Normandy invasion. The war will soon be carried beyond this place. It will rush toward Paris in the European Theater and is being enacted day by day with ferocity in the Pacific. But D-Day has changed the story altogether. Unless the remnants of the Axis have some stunning surprise—perhaps they get the bomb before we do?—the scales have irreversibly tipped. This astonishing and brilliant assault has succeeded. Setbacks are ahead. No one can control the weather, and no one could have foreseen the Battle of the Bulge, as we will shortly learn. But after D-Day, the Nazis are on the run and Hitler is bunkered. The Allies are free to properly honor their dead warriors in public.

ROBERT CAPA © INTERNATIONAL CENTER OF PHOTOGRAPHY/MAGNUM (2)

On to Berlin

The code names and nicknames—Slapstick, Overlord, D-Day—were in force before those operations were executed. None among the Allies anticipated, or would have wanted, what became known as the Battle of the Bulge.

By Daniel S. Levy

WORLD WAR II APPEARED TO BE ENDING. IN JULY 1944, Allied troops liberated Minsk, then a part of the Soviet Union, and the Majdanek concentration camp. In early August: Florence, Italy. Paris fell later in the month, troops marching down the Champs-Élysées and celebrating in the streets and cafés. Other cities and countries followed, from Athens and Luxembourg to Belgrade, Romania and Belgium. By early December, General Eisenhower, the Supreme Allied Commander in Europe, was told that the retreating Germans could not stage a major offensive, and he figured the war in Europe would be over by Christmas. It seemed just a matter of cleaning up.

But for Adolf Hitler, surrender was not an option. It didn't matter if his Third Reich was in tatters, if millions of Germans lay dead, if Allied bombers pulverized Berlin daily, if medieval cities and Renaissance palaces burned, if citizens were living in makeshift shelters, if they had to blow up the gas chambers and crematoriums at Auschwitz-Birkenau to destroy the evidence of the horror—and if the vengeful Soviet army was pushing forward from the east. Despite signs of defeat everywhere, suffering, Hitler believed, was ennobling—a test of the German spirit that would galvanize his people and lift them to glorious victory.

Hitler spent months planning one last assault, a final Blitzkrieg to match his brilliant lightning strike that had overwhelmed Poland and started the war in Europe in September 1939. The plan was to wait for the cover of overcast weather and then rush through the thinly guarded Ardennes Forest: wooded hills and valleys stretching from eastern Belgium through western Germany and into Luxembourg. German forces would then split and capture the Allied forces and take the port city of Antwerp. Hitler hoped that this devastating push would smash his enemy's line, destroy its will and force the foe to negotiate a fair peace.

To do this, Hitler's generals merged their battle-tested Waffen SS troops with a people's infantry made up of old men, young boys and criminals. Underground

GRANGER

Progress and Pain

On the previous pages, American GIs dash past disabled vehicles in a lane between hedgerows, heading toward nearby German positions during the fierce bocage fighting in Normandy on July 21, 1944. Some wars end when the vanquished know there is no clear way to victory, but this war against Adolf Hitler would not end that way. Above: American soldiers, sailors and Coast Guardsmen leave a ruined chapel near Omaha Beach after services on the first Sunday after D-Day. Left: Two women are on the run and take shelter from air raids during the Battle for Caen in France in mid-July. Opposite: In a photograph made on June 17, a bony horse grazes in a stable in Normandy—perhaps five miles from the beaches. In the foreground are German soldiers who have been killed in hand-to-hand combat.

BERLINER VERLAG/ARCHIV/PICTURE-ALLIANCE/DPA/AP

On to Berlin

factories hidden from the bombers cranked out weaponry for this bizarre hybrid army. The Germans stealthily massed 250,000 men—25 divisions—and waited.

It was quiet in the Ardennes; too quiet. With little for them to do, the sound of the falling snow and the frigid, whipping wind unsettled the 83,000 Americans strung along an 85-mile front. Some of the men, as well as a number of Belgian villagers, sensed something was up. Headquarters, though, told them they were being spooked by the breezes.

Then, at 5:30 on the morning of December 16, as clouds and drifting fog blanketed the valleys (preventing American planes from patrolling the area), a message was passed among the Germans: "Soldiers of the West Front! Your great hour has arrived." As *Unternehmen Wacht am Rhein*, Operation Watch on the Rhine—named for the German patriotic hymn—began, shells rained down on the Allies and German Panzer units and troops swarmed in, pushing

The Liberation of Paris

This was a great take-back in the summer of '44. Paris had twice been a target: for the Nazis, and now for the Allies. Below, left: An American tank is warmly welcomed by Parisians, relieved

to see the end of the German occupation. Below: There were at least two big liberation parades—August 26 and August 29—and this photograph taken in front of the Hôtel de Ville was probably made during the second liberation parade, when the American 28th Infantry was in town, American flags had been distributed and color film had been rolled into LIFE's cameras.

On to Berlin

through the American forces and creating a bulge in the Allied front. American troops were cut off, ran low on ammo, were attacked and surrounded. Some dug in and fought against the overwhelming wave. Forces retreated so fast they had to abandon their wounded to the care of medics. Others gave up, including some 7,000 men of the 106th Infantry Division, a surrender second in number of men only to that of the American forces at Bataan in the Philippines in April 1942. The Germans paraded the captured like trophies, and a demoralized Major General Alan Jones, said, "I've lost a division faster than any other commander in the U.S. Army."

While the assault took place, SS Lieutenant Colonel Otto Skorzeny—the scar-faced leader who had orchestrated the daring glider rescue of Benito Mussolini from the Hotel Campo Imperatore, high atop the Italian Gran Sasso Mountain, in September 1943—led a group of Greif commandos, English-speaking German soldiers who knew American slang and dressed in American uniforms, to spread confusion at the front. They captured American jeeps and carried out sabotage. Panic and confusion set in when the Americans discovered the infiltration. Soldiers at checkpoints interrogated troops to determine if they were really American: Did they know the name of President Franklin Roosevelt's dog (Fala) or Mickey Mouse's girl-friend (Minnie); who had won that year's World Series (the

Not According to Plan

After the success of D-Day, many of the Allied leaders assumed—or hoped—that the march to Berlin would be an easier effort, accompanied by casualties, certainly, but accomplished without inordinate resistance. Hitler had other ideas, and his counteroffensive, greatly abetted by bad weather, led to the Battle of the Bulge, an awful winter-season conflict that was frightful to fight and frightful in its consequences. Below: In July, before the bulge forms, the British leaders (from left, Lieutenant General Guy Simonds, Prime Minister Churchill, General Montgomery, and Lieutenant General Miles Dempsey) are in France confidently planning the way forward. The British had influence, certainly, but now the Americans were in charge of the strategy, which for a time seemed lost in the woods. Bottom: American soldiers in snowy forest in Amonines, Belgium, during the Battle of the Bulge.

BETTMANN/CORBIS

U.S. ARMY

THE BATTLE OF THE BULGE
DEC. 16, 1944–JAN. 25, 1945

From his "Wolf's Lair" headquarters in Rastenberg, East Prussia, Adolf Hitler perfected his master plan to win back the war, telling General Alfred Jodl that "I have made a momentous decision. I shall go over to the offensive . . . out of the Ardennes, with the objective Antwerp." He wanted his German troops to smash through the front the Allies had created since their D-Day landing and force them to negotiate for peace. Hitler insisted on this plan, scrawling "Not to Be Altered" on his order. Despite their doubts, his generals complied, and massed their tanks, artillery and men. Then in the early hours of December 16, they fired barrages of artillery, surged toward the overwhelmed American forces and pushed through the Allied front line, creating a bulge in the line as they headed for Antwerp. Fighting in the bitter cold and falling snow, the Germans made it to within sight of the Meuse River, but General Eisenhower regrouped his forces and pushed back against the German advance.

BELGIUM

A RIVER TOO FAR The Germans had set out with two dozen divisions, employing more than 2,600 tanks and assault guns. But by stretching 50 miles in, they were badly extended, low on supplies, and had to contend not only with the weather but with tanks and planes that Eisenhower poured into the fight.

ALLIED COUNTEROFFENSIVE
To counter the Germans, Eisenhower directed General Montgomery to lead his forces down from the north and the northwest, while General Bradley would head up from the south. At the same time, General Patton, who had been heading east into Germany, would shift his army north to the bulge. Just after Christmas he reached Bastogne to save the besieged 101st Airborne forces. Bradley's and Montgomery's men then met up in the town of Houffalize and closed the bulge.

WESTERN FRONT Six months after the Normandy invasion, the Ardennes Forest of Belgium and Luxembourg—an area of deep valleys, thick forests, rolling hills and sleepy towns—was the "quiet sector." Not expecting anything to happen there, the Allies stationed few troops along the 85-mile front. The Germans took advantage of this complacency.

NORTHERN OFFENSIVE In the misty woods, General Joseph "Sepp" Dietrich gathered his Sixth SS Panzer Army and spearheaded the assault toward the Meuse and then Antwerp, complaining as he did so: "All Hitler wants me to do is to cross a river, capture Brussels, and then go on and take Antwerp! And all this in the worst time of the year . . . when the snow is waist deep."

CENTER AND SOUTHERN OFFENSIVE In the center was General Hasso von Manteuffel with his Fifth Panzer Army to support Dietrich's left flank and head to St. Vith, Clairvaux and Wiltz. His troops assaulted the 101st Airborne at Bastogne, almost breached the Allied side and nearly reached the Meuse River. To the south, protecting Manteuffel's left flank, fought General Erich Brandenberger's Seventh Army.

Inset map labels: English Channel · Netherlands · ANTWERP · DÜSSELDORF · COLOGNE · BRUSSELS · Belgium · Germany · France · Battle of the Bulge · Lux. · Siegfried Line · Detail Area · PARIS · Allied Front Sept. 1944 · German Front · Miles 50 · km 50 100

Map labels: BRUSSELS · British First Army 21st Army Group General Montgomery commanding U.S. First and Ninth Armies · LIÈGE · Meuse River · SPA · U.S. 99th & 2nd Infantry Div. · U.S. 82nd Airborne Div. · MALMEDY · Elsenborn Ridge · Sixth Panzer Army · U.S. Ninth Army · U.S. VII Corps · Fifteenth Army · GERMANY · U.S. First Army · U.S. 7th AD · ST. VITH · U.S. 106 ID · 7,000 U.S. troops captured at Schnee Eifel · Fifth Panzer Army · DINANT · Dec. 25 · Dec. 20 · Dec. 16 · GIVET · Dec. 25 · ARDENNES · HOUFFALIZE · 28th ID · BITBURG · Seventh Army · BASTOGNE · 101st Airborne Div. · 9th AD · Dec. 25 · December 23–26 · Dec. 20 · 4th ID · LUX. · LUXEMBOURG · First Army · U.S. XVIII Airborne Division · FRANCE · 12th Army Group General Bradley · U.S. 4th Armored Division · U.S. III Corps · U.S. XII Corps · U.S. Third Army General Patton · METZ · 6th Army Group · N S E W · Miles 10 20 · km 10 20 30

MAP FOR LIFE BOOKS BY STEVE WALKOWIAK/SWMAPS.COM

The Battle of the Bulge

Below: An American Sherman M4 tank moves past a gun carriage that has slid off an icy road in the Ardennes Forest during a push to halt advancing German troops on December 20, 1944. Opposite: That same day, German prisoners of war are on grave-digging duty, five days before Christmas. History tells us that war is harsh. It has seldom been more harsh than during the Battle of the Bulge.

St. Louis Cardinals)? A soldier even stopped Omar Bradley, and though the general correctly answered that Springfield was the capital of Illinois, the MP believed it was Chicago, and held Bradley up until someone settled the confusion. American troops did not treat captured Greif soldiers mercifully: They were summarily shot.

Some Americans offered effective resistance. Near the village of Stavelot, Belgium, 13 men from a Combat Engineer Battalion stopped SS Colonel Joachim Peiper's Panzer line when their bazooka knocked off his lead tank. The Americans then took out three bridges across the Amblève and Salm Rivers. But by the second day the Allies realized that their four and a half divisions were badly overmatched by the assaulting German tanks, jeeps, trucks, troops and horses. Eisenhower and Bradley sent in reinforcements. One group, the 101st Airborne, raced to Bastogne to deny the Germans access to that market town's crucial network of roads and its clear path across the country. The men, told to hold on at all costs, dug in and prepared for an onslaught. Germans surrounded them, and clouds and falling snow on the twenty-first meant that American C-47s couldn't ferry in supplies.

On the morning of the twenty-second, Lieutenant Hellmuth Henke and three other Germans waving two white flags approached the Bastogne garrison. Henke yelled out, "We are parlementaires" and said they had a message laying out terms for surrender. The men, who came prepared with their own blindfolds, were led to a post, and their message was brought to Brigadier General Anthony C. McAuliffe. When the commander, whom his men fondly called "Old Crock," read the ultimatum, he said, "Us surrender? Aww, nuts!" His officers pointed out that he had to answer the Germans since they had brought a formal demand. McAuliffe looked at his staff and said, "Well, I don't know what to tell them." Lieutenant Colonel Harry

W.O. Kinnard responded, "What you said initially would be hard to beat." The staff agreed, and McAuliffe dispatched a typed note:

> *December 22, 1944*
> *To the German Commander,*
> *NUTS!*
> *The American Commander*

When Henke saw it he asked, "Is that reply negative or affirmative?" and Colonel Joseph "Bud" Harper told him, "The reply is decidedly not affirmative." The Germans still didn't understand, so Harper clarified that it meant "Go to hell."

The German response was to attempt annihilation. Artillery shells rained down and destroyed Bastogne as tanks and infantry assaulted. The Americans' supplies dwindled. They could not evacuate their wounded and had to use cognac as an anesthetic. But McAuliffe's gritty response had galvanized the men—a much-needed morale boost—and the fight was extended.

General George S. Patton's army, meanwhile, was pursuing the Germans at the Saar River to the south. He told Eisenhower that he could pivot troops and head to the

Onward

Yalta today is a resort city on the Black Sea in Ukraine. From February 4 to 11 in 1945, as part of the Soviet Union, it was the host of one of the most famous and consequential conferences of world leaders in history. On the opposite page we see a hearty Churchill, an infirm Roosevelt and a forward-looking Stalin sitting side by side during the Yalta photo op. They are relieved and thrilled, wary and worried, and very determined. They are perhaps each thinking about what has been achieved and—particularly with Stalin—what that might mean tomorrow. The achievements, in these last weeks in the European war, have included U.S. Ninth Army infantrymen progressing, under intense machine-gun and mortar fire, across a pontoon footbridge spanning the Roer River in Julich, Germany (the body of a comrade is in the foreground, right), and on March 26, German prisoners of war marching through the town of Limburg, Germany. The skies have cleared, the bulge is gone. The road to Berlin is open.

The Horror Revealed

Allied military personnel and western journalists now working their way through Germany and other European countries send word back down the lines: The rumors are true, and the atrocities are worse than can be imagined. The Third Reich had indeed been engaged in a systematic effort to exterminate the Jewish race. Photographers shooting for LIFE accompanied General Patton's Third Army as it liberated concentration camps in the spring of 1945, and Patton allowed them unfettered access—he wanted the world to know what had happened here. Photographer George Rodger made the image at right in April at Bergen-Belsen in northwestern Germany, and reported back of "dead lying by the side of one of the roads in the camp. They died like this in the thousands. There are piles of them among the pine trees. The SS guards gave them neither food nor water. When they became so weak they could no longer walk they just lay down and died, wherever they were." One of Margaret Bourke-White's most famous photos was made on April 13 at the liberation of Buchenwald (below). LIFE's editors later described these survivors "staring out at their Allied rescuers like so many living corpses." Opposite: That same spring, a dead soldier of the German Wehrmacht is pictured in front of Berlin's Brandenburg Gate.

GEORGE RODGER

MARGARET BOURKE-WHITE

134

bulge. And then, just before Christmas, like a gift from the heavens, the weather cleared and planes were able to go in and fire at the German tanks and troops. Patton's army roared into Bastogne the day after Christmas, rescued the 101st, and the warrior dubbed "Old Blood and Guts" pinned a Distinguished Service Cross on McAuliffe.

The battle took a heavy toll on the Allies, and by Christmas the U.S. Army had lost 4,000 men, with 30,000 wounded or captured. The Germans treated prisoners viciously. On December 17, more than 100 American soldiers surrendered to SS Colonel Peiper's men. The Germans disarmed them and gathered them in a field near Malmédy. A few escaped. But those who didn't were gunned down. The Germans then clubbed to death the men who didn't die right away. They also shot Belgians they suspected of harboring Americans. In and around the town of Stavelot, Peiper's troops killed more than 100 men, women and children.

HEINRICH HOFFMANN/TIME LIFE PICTURES/GETTY

The German offensive, which had created a 50-mile-deep bulge, stalled just a few miles from the Meuse River. With the Germans stopped, Eisenhower closed the space between his armies. Regrouping in late December, he gave Montgomery command of the northern sector and Bradley the southern sector, then set out to squeeze the two sides of the bulge together and push the Germans east. The Allies in Europe had a clear advantage over their Nazi foes, a 10-to-1 superiority in tanks, three times the aircraft and two and a half times as many men. Eisenhower sent in a half million more troops, many of them green, untested recruits who arrived ill prepared for what awaited. They were told that most of them weren't coming back and they should just get used to the idea.

The fight continued to be long and hard. The Germans, now on the defensive, overextended and badly exposed, tried to keep an opening to get their men out of the bulge and back across the Rhine to Germany. The winter of 1944 to 1945 was the most severe in memory, and theirs was a hard retreat. They fought as they went, setting up positions in towns and in elevated areas when they could. American

WILLIAM VANDIVERT

troops had to capture one town at a time, with howitzers shelling the homes and men shooting their way in.

NAPOLEON ONCE SAID THAT "THE FIRST QUALITY IN A soldier is constancy in enduring fatigue and hardship. Courage is only second. Poverty, privation

The Bitter End

Opposite, top: On April 20, 1945, in the last authenticated photograph made of Hitler, the German leader greets members of the Hitler Youth brigade as they prepare to defend Berlin. Opposite, bottom: In May, Hitler's command center conference room has been partially burned out by SS troops and stripped of evidence by invading Russians. It is part of the famous bunker where Hitler, 56, had committed suicide on April 30. Above: On May 7 in Reims, France, General Eisenhower shares news of the German surrender.

137

and want are the school of the good soldier." This is what it was like for the Americans and Germans both. The winter wind and biting, blinding snow confused all combatants. There was often limited visibility, and Americans even fired on their comrades. Frozen bodies littered the ground. Men stuck out in the open tried to break through the frozen earth to make foxholes, chipping away at the snow and ice, pulling logs over the holes for protection from the screaming artillery shells. They were given whiskey to stay warm. Cold and exhausted men huddled together to sleep and preserve body heat. Many of the wounded slowly bled to death, their companions incapable of getting them help. When troops came out from cover for an assault, they had to rush through open, snow-covered fields, their clear figures easily picked off by German infantrymen and artillery.

The push forward was hard, and the battle strained relations between Eisenhower and the abrasive Montgomery, who wanted control of all American forces. Monty's attitude so infuriated Ike that he wanted to fire him, and when news of the tensions arrived at Hitler's headquarters, it gladdened the Führer.

Fighting decimated towns. Citizens, huddling in cellars, had little food. They prayed. Some ventured out to bring back snow; when it melted, the desperately needed drinking water was often blackened by the residue of gunpowder and exploded shells.

The town of Houffalize, Belgium, was chosen by Eisenhower for a rendezvous of the two Allied armies. The Americans pummeled that community. Patton observed that "the mental attitude of the men was excellent. Heretofore they had been somewhat dubious; now they were chasing a sinking fox and babbling for the kill." Houffalize fell, but fighting continued until the end of the month just to recoup the last 10 miles, with the Allies finally returning to where they had started in mid-December.

Hollow-eyed men slogged on. They had to keep moving

forward, moving forward, moving forward. Boots were worn down, ripped, and the wet, cold slog turned feet numb. Many developed trench foot. As feet swelled, they turned black and then blue. If gangrene could not be controlled, surgeons amputated toes and feet. Doctors patched up the wounded as best they could, recycled penicillin from urine and tapped healthy men for transfusions. Some soldiers cracked from the stress of combat: shell shock. Doctors prescribed them sodium amytal, pills they called "Blue 88s" after the feared German 88mm antiaircraft artillery pieces, and tried to get them to snap out of it. If that quick and dirty remedy worked, the soldiers received a pep talk and were sent back to the front.

As their retreat collapsed, German officers shot men who tried to surrender to the Allies. By the end of January, the situation arrived back to where the battle had started six weeks earlier. By then, 19,000 Americans were dead, 70,000 wounded or captured, making the Battle of the Bulge the bloodiest battle for the United States in the war. The Germans suffered many times that number of casualties.

The victorious Allies now had their final objective clearly in sight. They pointed their planes, their tanks, their jeeps and their men east and headed toward Hitler's smoldering capital, Berlin.

Aftermath

They began building a graveyard above Omaha Beach to bury the famous men killed in Normandy (Brigadier General Theodore Roosevelt Jr., Lieutenant General Lesley McNair) . . . and the many who remained anonymous. There would be 9,387 graves in the American cemetery, and later General Eisenhower and his wife, Mamie, pay respects at the grave of an unknown soldier (opposite). As for World War II's vanquished: There would be judgment. Above: In October 1946 at the International Military Tribunal held in the German city of Nuremberg are, in the front row from left, Hermann Göring, Rudolf Hess, Joachim von Ribbentrop and Wilhelm Keitel, guarded by military police as they listen to the evidence against them. Behind, from left, are Karl Dönitz, Erich Raeder, Baldur von Schirach and Fritz Sauckel. These are eight of 21 former leaders of the Third Reich facing their judges in what one of the British jurists taking part, Norman Birkett, called "the greatest trial in history." Of these defendants, Dönitz received 10 years; von Schirach, 20; and Hess and Raeder got life sentences. The other four were condemned to death, but Göring committed suicide with a hidden potassium cyanide capsule on the night before his scheduled execution. The Russians had wanted to hold the trial in Berlin, but Nuremberg was selected at least in part because it was seen as the spiritual birthplace of the Nazis, where once they had staged their mass rallies. So where this horrible chapter in world history began, there it now ended.

"Taps"

Seventy years later, the men and memories of June 6, 1944,
linger in Normandy. They ever will.

Photographs by Harry Benson

Calm Long After the Storm The Côte du Bessin was code-named Omaha Beach in Allied plans and became the venue for ferocious fighting,
Today, it is becalmed, though the scars of battle can still be seen.

It has become, perhaps, the most poignant piece of music ever written. Other balladic compositions by the great masters are perhaps "better," but when one hears "Taps," the emotions—and thoughts—are stirred. The bugler falters on the sixth note at the President's funeral. Who would not?

But there is general misunderstanding. "Taps" doesn't indicate, simply, death—though the piece is often played at military funerals. "Taps" is also known as "Butterfield's Lullaby"—a beautiful title—or "Day Is Done," three words that are the centerpiece of the first line of its original lyric (and, yes, "Taps" does have lyrics). It is not only played graveside, it has been sounded at campfires around which sit Boy or Girl Scouts, and at 10,000 flag-lowering ceremonies around the globe. *Day Is Done.*

Finally, 70 years ago, D-Day was done.

Brigadier General Daniel Butterfield was awarded the Medal of Honor for his service in the Union Army during America's Civil War. He was commander of the 3rd Brigade of the 1st Division of the V Army Corps of the Army of the Potomac. In July 1862, after the ferocious Seven Days battles, in which he and 600 of his men were casualties, Butterfield asked for a new song to replace the austere French bugle call for "lights out" then in use. The brigade's bugler, Oliver Willcox Norton, obeyed orders: "[S]howing me some notes on a staff written in pencil on the back of an envelope, [General Butterfield] asked me to sound them on my bugle. I did this several times, playing the music as written. He changed it somewhat, lengthening some notes and shortening others, but retaining the melody as he first gave it to me. After getting it to his satisfaction, he directed me to sound that call for 'Taps' thereafter in place of the regulation call. The music was beautiful on that still summer night and was heard far beyond the limits of our Brigade. The next day I was visited by several buglers from neighboring Brigades, asking for copies of the music, which I gladly furnished. The call was gradually taken up through the Army of the Potomac." Thus was "Taps" first and forevermore sounded, in short order taken up by Union and, later, Confederate forces. Since its initial playing, "Taps" has fairly cried out the words *elegy* and *tribute* and *farewell* and *gratefulness* . . . and *good night.*

On the beaches of Normandy today, 70 years after the fearsome facts, all of the memories are preserved. In these last five pages of our book, they are preserved by the photographer Harry Benson, who has been contributing to LIFE since the 1960s. When you walk those beaches, you hear "Taps" clearly, although there is no trumpeter within miles.

Read with us now the original words. Although they were written long before D-Day by Horace Lorenzo Trim, they spoke—and speak—to what would become D-Day.

> *Day is done, gone the sun*
>
> *From the lakes, from the hills, from the sky*
> *All is well, safely rest*
> *God is nigh.*
>
> *Fading light dims the sight*
> *And a star gems the sky, gleaming bright*
> *From afar, drawing near*
> *Falls the night.*
>
> *Thanks and praise for our days*
> *Neath the sun, neath the stars, neath the sky*
> *As we go, this we know*
>
> *God is nigh.*

© HARRY BENSON

with the Allies storming ashore and the Germans on high, firing down.

The High Ground

This barbed wire is still visible atop Pointe du Hoc, the 100-foot cliff that is the highest point between what were code-named Utah Beach and Omaha Beach, and a position for German artillery—and trickery. On D-Day, the U.S. Army Ranger Assault Group climbed the cliff and had to surmount this wire to advance. Opposite, from top: The view from inside a German bunker overlooking Omaha Beach; the view from the beach, looking at such bunkers; a wooden cross dedicated to the Germans killed at Omaha.

© HARRY BENSON (4)

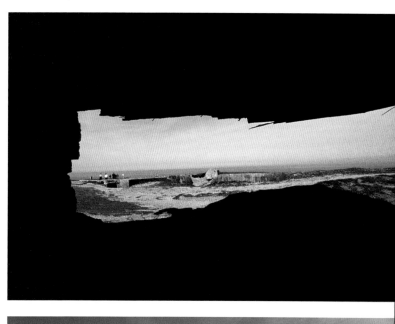

© HARRY BENSON

Rest in Peace

Seventy years on . . . the battle that changed—perhaps saved—the world. So many died, so many of them so bravely. Here is the Normandy American Cemetery and Memorial near Colleville-sur-Mer, France. It honors all of the United States servicemen who died in World War II and was begun immediately, in June 1944. There are 9,387 American war dead buried here.